Facial Asymmetry in Expression of Emotion

About the Auther

Dr. H.S. Asthana obtained his degrees of M.A. (Psychology) and Ph.D. (Psychology) specialising in Clinical Neuropsychology from Banaras Hindu University. Having served Administrative Training Institute, Nainital and various Universities for example Gurukul Kangri University, Haridwar, Kumaun University, Nainital and Indira Gandhi National Open University, New Delhi with over 15 years of experience is presently working as Associate Professor, Department of Psychology, Banaras Hindu University, Varanasi.

He has authored one text-book and published about 30 research papers. He completed two projects funded by CSIR and UGC besides getting honour of Young Scientist Award.

Facial Asymmetry in Expression of Emotion

A NEUROCULTURAL PERSPECTIVE

Dr. H. S. Asthana
Associate Professor, Deptt. of Psychology,
Banaras Hindu University, Varanasi-221005

CONCEPT PUBLISHING COMPANY PVT. LTD.
NEW DELHI-110059

Facial Asymmetry in Expression

ISBN-13 : 978-81-8069-847-7

First Published 2012

Published and Printed by

Concept Since 1974

Concept Publishing Company Pvt. Ltd.
A/15-16, Commercial Block, Mohan Garden
New Delhi-110059 (India)
T: 25351460, 25351794, *F*: 091-11-25357109
E: publishing@conceptpub.com, W: www.conceptpub.com
Editorial Office: H-13, Bali Nagar, New Delhi-110 015, India.

Cataloging in Publication Data--*Courtesy:* D.K. Agencies (P) Ltd. <docinfo@dkagencies.com>

Asthana, H. S.
Facial asymmetry in expression of emotion : a neurocultural perspective / H.S. Asthana.
p. cm.
Includes bibliographical references (p.) and index.
ISBN 9788180698477

1. Facial expression. 2. Emotions. 3. Neuropsychology. I. Title.

DDC 153.69 23

Preface

Expression of emotion has been a long studied issue in the field of psychology. It has great impact on people when they are expressed in such a way that can be perceived by others. Among the different channels, the facial expression is regarded as most important channel of expression of emotion because human face provides useful information on the emotion and the inner state of the individual. Although, there is no doubt that certain facial expressions are universal in nature. Opinion however differs in regard to the fact that these emotions are modulated to some extent depending upon the culture specific norms. There are two contrary views regarding this context. The first one is that facial expression and emotion labels are probably associated but the association may vary with culture. The second one is that facial expression might be innate (but not displayed in adults cultures) or universal because of culture constant learning. On the other hand, Ekman proposed Neuro-cultural theory of facial expression of emotion. It suggests that expressions of fundamental emotions are stored in Facial Affect Programme and culture specific display rules modulate these expressions to some extent depending on social context. So, Ekman's theory of facial expression of emotion emphasizes cultural differences as well as universality.

Little attempt has been made to empirically examine the theory with interdependence of neuronal and cultural component since they are closely intertwined. One possibility in this direction is to apply the phenomenon of facial asymmetry to isolate the facial side that is more governed by the social display rules and the side that is predominantly under the influence of innate biological system. Therefore, in the present study a neuropsychological approach has been adopted to isolate the neuronal and cultural component of facial expression of emotion. It carries both the theoretical and applied significance. The theoretical significance is related to the empirical validation of neuro-cultural theory of expression of emotion, whereas applied significance reveals the role of social display rules in interpersonal relationship.

The present book is the outcome of the UGC funded research project to the author in the name of Kumaun University. I am extremely thankful to the University Grants Commission, New Delhi for providing financial assistance to carry out the present empirical study.

It is with profound gratitude and esteem reverence, I express my sincere thanks to Professor M.K. Mandal, Director, DIPR, DRDO, New Delhi for providing the standardized sets of photographs as a tool of the project and providing.valuable suggestions. I owe a great debt to Dr. Sunita Asthana and Pooja Asthana for their lot of encouragement and their support. I express my gratitude to all of them who participated in this study but could not be mentioned.

H.S. Asthana

Contents

Introduction

Origin of Research

Expression of emotion has been a long studied issue in the field of psychology. Emotions have great impact on people when they are expressed outwardly in ways that can be perceived by others. Different researches have defined the term emotion in different ways. For example a cultural definition, a definition on the basis of overt expression, a psychobiological definition of emotion etc.

Generally, by the term emotion, we refer to reactions to appropriately evocative situation involving perception, appraisal, subjectively experienced feelings, autonomic and neural arousal, expressive behaviour and goal directed activity. Among these aspects, perceptions and external expressions are more important in non-verbal communication. For effective non-verbal communication both the sending accuracy i.e. ability to express emotion that could reflect the actual feeling of the individual and the receiving ability i.e. ability to judge the emotional state of the individual must be present to a greater extent.

Historically, emotional behaviour in linked with subcortical/ limbic structures such as the lower portion of the brain stem, diencephalon, thalamus, and limbic system. The role neocortex has recently been emphasized. The present work is primarily based on hemispheric superiority/specialization in expression of facial emotion.

Before discussing the literature on hemispheric involvement in the expression of facial emotion, it is important to discuss the importance of facial channel over other different channels of communication. There are three important channels of communication which have been studied— prosodic, lexical and facial. Prosodic channel helps in communicating the emotional tone of the spoken content (such as melody, accent, etc.). The verbal content of the speech is communicated through lexical channel.

The facial channel is most widely studied in neuropsychological researches because of the following reasons:

(1) The kind and content of information it conveys is relatively easy to comprehend.

(2) The human face provides many useful informations regarding emotion and inner state of the individual.

(3) The face is rich in communicative potential.

(4) It is the primary site for communicating emotional state.

(5) Further facial muscles have fibre connections with subcortical and cortical structures.

(6) Finally, the face is exposed to the full view of others for the facility of social interaction. This is the reason of choosing the facial channel of expressing emotion as a stimulus.

In general, people are less aware of the differential involvement of the two sides of face during expression of emotion. This behaviour is termed as facedness or facial asymmetry. The term facial asymmetry refers to the fact that the left and right sides of human face during rest or movement are not identical. The facedness is measured or perceived in terms of the relative intensity of expression and the extent of muscular involvement on the left and right sides of the face. Before discussing the literature on facial asymmetry, it is essential to discuss the neuroanatomical substrates of facial expression of emotion as well as methodological considerations in the studies of facial asymmetry.

Neuroanatomical Substrates of Facial Expression

The muscles of the face are composed of two groups—the mastication muscles and the expressive or mimic muscles. On each side of the face, there are four muscles. These are temprails, the masseter, and the internal and external petryoid muscles (Rinn,1984). Motor neurons of the brain that innervate facial muscles are of two types: the upper motor neurons that send impulses from the motor centre of the cortex to the brain stem and/or spinal cord and the lower motor neurons that send impulses from the brain stem/spinal cord to the facial muscles (Rinn,1984). The lower motor neuron tract that provides major motor innervation of the muscles of facial expression is known as the facial nerve or seventh cranial nerve (Brodal, 1965; Miehlke, 1973).

Neuroanatomical literature suggests relatively independent neuroanatomical pathways for posed and spontaneous facial expressions. For example, posed expressions are governed by the pyramidal tracts of the facial nerves that descend from the cortex. Spontaneous expressions, on the other hand, are governed by the extra-pyramidal tracts of the subcortical origin

(Van Gelder, 1981; cited in Borod and Koff, 1990). Although there is some consensus on the fact that facial nerves of pyramidal tracts are contra-laterally distributed to the lower region of the face (Borod and Koff, 1984; Campbell, 1986), opinion differs on the precise nature of the neuronal distribution in the upper face. With regard to spontaneous expression, there is little consensus about the neuronal pathways (crossed or uncrossed) that are distributed to the upper or lower regions of the face.

Methodological Considerations

Two common methods, judgmental and anatomical/ electrophysiological are available to measure facial behaviour. Most investigators have utilized the judgmental method to study facial asymmetry. In this method, observer's judgment is considered as the dependent and facial behaviour as the independent measure. Based on observer's judgment, facial behaviours are calibrated and inferences are drawn (Ekman, 1982). In the studies of facial asymmetry, the judgmental method is used with a variety of stimuli, for example, symmetrical composite faces, hemiregional composite face, videotapes of whole faces and hemifaces.

(A) Symmetrical Composite Faces from Photographic Stills

This method entails preparation of facial composites by cutting the original and mirror reversed print of each photograph along the vertical midline (e.g. Sackeim and Gur, 1978). The left-left composite is thus prepared by joining the left hemiface of normal orientation and its mirror image. Similarly, the Right-Right (RR) facial composite is prepared by assembling the right hemiface of normal orientation and its mirror image. Observers are asked to rate these composite photographs in terms of intensity of its expression.

(B) Hemiregional Composite Faces from Photographic Stills

To develop hemiregional composite photographs, first hemifacial composites are prepared. These composites are then cut along the horizontal mid-line bisecting the upper (forehead, brows, eyes and root of the nose) and lower (lower part of the nose, cheeks, mouth and chin) regions of face. The lower part of the left facial composite (LL) is then joined with the upper part of the Right-Right (RR) to produce the RR/LL hemiregional composite and *vice versa* to get the LL/RR composite. Observers are asked to rate/rank these hemiregional composite photographs in terms of expressed intensity.

(C) Videotapes of Whole Faces and Hemifaces

In this approach, participants' expressions are videotaped during different conditions of emotional expressions. These videotaped clips are then presented in either a dynamic or static mode for participants' rating in terms of intensity or muscular movement.

The utilization of the electro-physiological/anatomical method in the study of facial asymmetry is reported rather less often. In the electro-physiological methods, such as EMG recording (Giard, Tassinary, Kappas and Bontempo,1996; Girard, Tassinary, Kappas, Gosselin and Bontempo,1997), muscle actions in the face are measured. The anatomical methods are based on distinct facial muscle movements that are coded in terms of action units, such as FAST (Ekman, Friesen, and Tomkins, 1971), FACS (Ekman and Friesen, 1978) or MAX (Izard, 1983). This measurement technique requires the EMG lead to be placed over facial areas that are expected to be differentially active for emotion studied. Surface electromyographic measurements are sensitive to differences among recalled emotions (Schwartz *et al.*, 1976). Asymmetry in the EMG of Zygomatic muscles is used as an indicator of facial asymmetry (Schwartz, Ahern and Brown, 1979).

Facial Action Scoring Technique (FAST)

In this technique experimenters observe separate areas of the hemiface for visible facial movement, which are then compared with standard photographic examples (Ekman, Friesen, and Tomkins, 1971). The difference in hemifacial movement with standard photographic examples substantiates the notion of facial asymmetry.

Facial Action Coding System (FACS)

The FACS (Ekman and Friesen, 1978) is designed to measure each visible facial behaviour in any context. This system isolates all anatomically based muscle measurement during emotional expression and action units are identified. Facial asymmetry is studied in terms of action units on each hemiface (Hager and Ekman, 1985).

Maximally Discriminative Facial Movements Coding System (MAX)

The MAX (Izard, 1983) was developed to objectively measure organized pattern of facial movements or appearance changes that signal human emotions. Unlike other anatomical coding systems (like FACS), MAX was designed to examine facial behaviour in young and preverbal children. Facial asymmetry is measured in terms of different codes representing appearance changes.

Review of Literature

Darwin (1872) was the first to point out that two sides of human face are not equally expressive. However, the first systematic study of facial asymmetry was conducted by Lynn and Lynn (1938). They have used the term facedness to characterize facial asymmetry during emotional or non-emotional expressions. Wolff (1943) studied facial asymmetry from an emotional quality point of view and reported that right side of the human face offers social or public expressions where the left hemiface reveals hidden and personalized feeling.

Asymmetry in facial expressions has been studied from still photographs and videotapes, and investigators have attempted to examine hemifacial asymmetry during posed facial emotion. Campbell (1978) used composite faces of nine different expressions depicting the happy (smile) emotion. He found that the left hemiface was judged to be expressing happiness more intensely than the right hemiface. Sackein and Gur (1978) used composite faces posing six different emotions and a neutral expression. Participants rated each composite photograph on a 7 point-scale of expressed intensity. The left side composites were judged as expressing emotion more intensely than the right composites. In a somewhat different methodology, observers were asked to rate left-left and right-right facial composites with bipolar adjectives. Results revealed that left-left composites were rated as 'healthier, stronger, harder, more active, and more excitable'. In contrast, right-right composites were rated as sickly, weaker, more feminine, more passive and calmer (Karch and Grant, 1978).

In a study, Borod, Caron and Koff (1981) have utilized videotaped facial expression of whole face and judges were asked to rate each expression for the degree of facial asymmetry. The left hemiface was judged as significantly more involved in facial expression than the right hemiface. Borod and her associates substantiated the notion on many occasions in later studies. These studies revealed that the left hemifacial composite was judged to have depicted greater affective tone than that of the right hemiface (Borod, Kent, Koff, Martin, and Alpert, 1988; Borod and Koff, 1990; Borod, St. Clair, Koff and Alpert, 1990). Support for the left hemifacial bias during expression was obtained from other studies as well (Asthana and Mandal, 1997; 1998; Baribiane *et al.*,1987; Mandal *et al.*, 1993; Moreno *et al.*, 1990; see also review, Asthana, Bhushan and Mandal, 2000; Borod, Haywood and Koff, 1997; Mandal, Asthana, and Biswal, 2008). The greater left hemifacial dominance in expression of emotion has been interpreted as right hemispheric dominance because each side of the face, especially lower two-third part is controlled by the contralateral hemisphere (De Jong, 1979).

Some studies, however, have failed to demonstrate systematic left-facedness during posed expression of emotion. Knox (1972) employed lateral half face in a study in which observers were asked to judge which half face was expressing happiness more intensely. There was no significant difference in the judgment of the two sides of face. Others, however, have reported left facedness in the expression of happiness (Campbell, 1979; Kowner, 1995). In a study, Cacioppo and Petty (1981) also found no evidence of facial asymmetry. The absence of facial asymmetry is supported in other studies also (for example, Kop, Merckelbach, and Muris, 1991; Schwartz, Ahern, and Brown, 1979; Sirota and Schwartz, 1982). Ladavas (1982) reported that left facial asymmetries are found in older but not in younger groups (age 12-23 years) during posed expressions of emotions.

In most of the studies hemifacial asymmetry in expression of emotion has been investigated by utilizing either symmetric facial composite photographs or with chimeric faces. Although, Neuroanatomical literature to some extent suggests the left-right as well as upper-lower facial differences in terms of behavioural pattern and neural innervations (Ekman and Friesen, 1975; Rinn, 1984), but no systematic attempt has been made to examine the proposition empirically. Asthana and Mandal (1997), conducted an experiment to examine the role of left-right as well as upper-lower regions of the face during posed emotional expression with a modification in a composite-photograph methodology. The hemiregional composites (RR/LL and LL/RR) were prepared by bisecting the left-left and right-right composites into upper and lower regions to produce composites of upper right-right and lower left-left (RR/LL) and upper left-left and lower right-right (LL/RR) facial parts. Such hemiregional composites provide an opportunity to examine the differential role of upper and lower regions in addition to left-right hemifaces during an emotional expression. The hemiregional composites of facial expression involving RR/LL were judged as most expressive followed by left hemifacial composites. This finding was further verified in other study also (Asthana and Ahmed, 2005). This finding suggests that the left hemifacial involvement was specific to the lower region and the right hemifacial involvement was specific to the upper regions during emotional expression. On the basis of this finding, it has been speculated that the upper region of the face is probably controlled by ipsilateral rather than contralateral fibre connections.

Facial Asymmetry and Emotional Valence

Although much of the current literature suggests left facedness, that is, superiority of the right hemisphere in the expression of facial emotion. On the other hand, many researchers have reported a differential facial involvement for emotion as a function of emotional valence (Ehrlichman, 1987; Sackeim, Greenberg, Weiman, Gur, Hungerbuhler, and Geschwind, 1982). The valence hypothesis proposes that negative emotions are predominantly associated with the right hemisphere and positive emotions with the left hemisphere (see reviews by Leventhal and Tomarken, 1986; Tucker, 1981). Studies on the valence hypothesis carried out by Borod and associates (Borod and Caron, 1980; Borod *et al.*, 1983; Borod *et al.*, 1988) indicated left facedness for negative emotions (a finding that was supported by Mandal and Singh, 1990; Sackeim and Grega, 1987; Schiff and Lamon, 1989; Wemple *et al.*, 1986) and for positive emotions, both hemifaces were found equally expressive (a finding that was supported by Hagar and Ekman, 1985; Schiff and Lamon, 1989). On the other hand, some researchers have reported right facedness for positive emotions. (Brockmeier and Ulrich, 1993; Schiff and MacDonald, 1990). In a study, Yecker, Borod, Brozgold, Martin, Alpert and Welkowitz (1999) reported that approach expressions were more left-sided.

A meta-analytic study by Skinner and Mullen (1991) reported that left hemiface expresses emotion more intensely than the right hemiface. This asymmetry was more pronounced for negative emotion than for positive emotion. Left-sided asymmetries were more frequent for negative (100%) than for positive (76%) emotional expression. Right-sided asymmetries were more frequent for positive (24%) than for negative (10%) emotional expressions (Borod, 1993: 457).

Borod (1992: 341) had two speculations in favour of this finding:

1. Negative emotions are linked to a survival mechanism, thereby requiring a Gestalt or synthetic processing (a function of the RH).
2. Positive emotions are more linguistic/communicative than emotional; thus a relative dominance of the LH is more evident.

In recent times, a great deal of attention has been paid to the issues of the hemifacial asymmetry and culture-specificity of facial expression of emotion. There is little doubt that certain facial expressions of emotion are universal in nature such as crying and smiling. Opinions however differ in regard to the fact that these emotions are modulated to some extent depending upon the culture specific norms.

Review of the reviews in this context has shown contradictory argument (Ekman, 1994; Izard, 1994; Russell, 1994). For example, Russell (1994) concluded that—"facial expression and emotion label are probably associated but the association may vary with culture". On the other hand, Izard (1994) suggested that facial expression might be innate (but not displayed in adults of all cultures) or universal because of culture constant learning. Ekman (1994) in support of his neurocultural theory maintained that expression of fundamental emotions are stored in an Facial Affect Programme and culture specific display rules (For example: neutralizing/deintensifying the appearance of a felt emotion or masking it with the configuration of another emotion) modulate these expressions to some extent depending on social context. Neurocultural theory of emotion provides comprehensive framework for studying universal and cultural differences in facial expression. This theory suggests that universality in facial expression occurs through the operation of facial affect programme which specifies the relationship between distinctive movement of facial muscles and particular emotions. Cultural differences in facial expression occur: (a) because the eliciting events that call an emotion usually vary across culture, (b) because the display rules vary across culture. Mastumoto (1992) found a statistical significant interaction between culture and the type of facial expression. In fact, Ekman's Neuro-cultural theory of facial expression of emotion emphasizes cultural differences as well as universality. The theory postulates that facial expressions are triggered by an innate facial programme but may be masked, intensified or neutralized to suit the shared norms in a given culture. Little attempt has been made to test the theory with interdependence of neuronal and cultural component, since they are closely intertwined. In fact, most expressions of facial emotions across culture are modulated to a great extent. For example, Japanese generally mask their negative emotional feelings with smiling (Friesen, 1972; cited in Mastumoto, 1990); oriental Indians tend to deintensify the negatively charged emotions fear, anger) (Mandal, Bryden, and Bulman-Fleming, 1996).

In most of the studies, posed facial expressions are used (Levenson, Ekman, and Friesen, 1990) because spontaneous expressions are difficult to elicit for scientific purpose as well as in fact, in any given social situation, pure, uninhibited emotions are rarely expressed facially (Russell, 1994).

Therefore, posed expressions are used to investigate universality vs. culture specific issues. Posed expressions which are elicited either by muscle instruction or by the instruction to create face by imagining a situation, are also not free from learned components. It was found that voluntarily performing certain facial muscular actions generated involuntary changes in autonomic nervous system activity (Ekman, 1992). Ekman, however argued that (1) the changes in an ANS activity may be unique to the specific task (rather than specific to emotion) and (2) any connection between expression and physiological change may be learned not hard wired (Ekman, 1992). One possibility in this direction is to isolate the facial side that is more governed by the social display rules and the side that is predominantly under the influence of innate biological system. To isolate these two components a neuropsychological approach would be most appropriate.

Review of neuropsychological literature on facial asymmetry suggest that two sides of human face are not equally expressive (see review by Asthana, Bhushan, and Mandal, 2000; Borod, Haywood and Koff, 1997). Wolff (1943) suggested that the right side of the face is more under conscious control revealing interpersonally meaningful expressions (public) whereas the left side of the face is under unconscious control revealing mostly hidden emotions (private).

Asthana, Mandal and Pandey (1992) partially supported Wolff's proposition. It was hypothesized that we learn in course of human development to civilise intense emotional expression of subcortical origin by the side of the face (right) which is more under the voluntary control of relatively less emotional side of the cerebral hemisphere (i.e. left) for the facility of social interaction (Asthana and Mandal, 1996). Buck (1984) has suggested that the right hemisphere (left hemiface) is associated with general affective or emotional processes and left hemisphere (right hemiface) with the control of these processes according to social display rules. Expressions of the left side of the face are less influenced by the display rules and expressions of the right side of the face would be less pronounced as learned display rules may miniaturize, suppress, or temporarily abbreviate (Izard, 1994) emotional signals to conform to social norms.

Cultural display norms for facial expressions are believed to be influenced to a great extent by the sex of the expresser (Buck, Baron, and Barrette,1982; Buck, Baron, Goodman, and Shapiro, 1980) and the emotion category (Russell, 1991). In a study, Mandal, Harizuka, Bhushan and Mishra (2001) have examined the role of cultural variations in hemifacial expression.

With this background, it is clearly evident that little attempt has been made to examine the effect of cultural differences in hemifacial expression of emotion. Further researches are needed with modifications in the stimuli as well as methodology to arrive at any conclusion regarding the universality and culture specific issues on hemifacial expression of emotion.

Objectives of the Study

Therefore, the present study was intended to examine the differential role of cultural display norms on facial asymmetry in expression of emotion by utilizing hemifacial and hemi-regional facial composites with methodological refinement.

The prime objective of the present study was to examine whether culture display rules of three different cultures (i.e. Indian, American and Japanese) differentially influence to different hemifaces, valence of emotion and sex of expressors during expression of facial emotion.

The specific objectives are given below:

(1) To examine the hemifacial and hemiregional asymmetry/variations in the expression of facial emotion.

(2) To examine the hemifacial and hemiregional asymmetry with respect to the sex of the expressor and valence of emotion.

(3) To examine the interaction between the culture and valence of emotion with respect to different facial composites.

(4) To examine the role of culture display rules with respect to left-right hemifaces, valence of emotion and sex of the expressors.

Hypotheses

To fulfil the objectives of the study the following alternative hypotheses were formulated:

(I) The hemiregional facial composites involving upper right-right and lower left-left part (RR/LL) would be most expressive in terms of intensity of expression of emotion than any other hemiregional and hemifacial composites.

(II) Left hemiface would be more expressive than the right hemiface in expression of facial emotion.

(III) Right hemiface would be more influenced by the cultural/social display rules of expression of facial emotion, than the left hemiface.

(IV) Expression of negative emotions would be more influenced by cultural display rules of emotion expression than positive emotions.

(V) Expression of negatively aroused emotions would be more influenced by cultural display rules of expression of emotion than the negatively non-aroused emotions.

(VI) Female expressors would be more influenced by the cultural display rules of expression of facial emotion than male expressors attain the objectives of the study and to test the hypotheses empirically altogether three different experiments were conducted.

Experiment 1

The first experiment was primarily intended to examine the first two hypotheses of the study. These hypotheses are:

(1) The hemiregional facial composite involving upper right-right and lower left-left (RR/LL) would be more expressive in terms of intensity of expression of emotion than any other hemiregional and hemifacial composites.

(2) Left hemiface would be more expressive than the right hemiface in terms of its expression of facial emotion.

METHODOLOGY

Subjects

Altogether 125 (Mean Age 28.5 yrs (±5.2 yrs); Mean Education (12.2 yrs) subjects between the age of 20 to 40 years were selected from the different regions of Uttarakhand like Almora, Nainital, Haldwani, Pithoragarh and Haridwar for participation in the Experiment 1. Since handedness is considered an important factor to influence neuropsychological researches, the hand preference of each subject was assessed by using Hand Preference Schedule (Mandal, Pandey, Singh, and Asthana, 1992). Subjects with a hand preference quotient below +.25 were not included in the study sample (range left always –1.00

to right always +1.00). Therefore, all participants were clearly right-handed.

Subjects with a history of hand change were not considered. Information regarding familial handedness was also obtained. Subjects with (a) impaired sighting performance and (b) history of brain disease were also excluded from the study sample.

Tool

Three standardized sets of facial photographs depicting six fundamental emotions: happy, sad, fear, anger, surprise and disgust were used in the present study. These three sets of photographs were the pictures of facial affect developed by:

(a) Mandal (1987) based on Indian expressors;
(b) Ekman and Friesen (1976) with American expressors; and
(c) Mandal, Harizuka, Bhushan and Mishra (2001) with Japanese expressors.

The photographs of each set are standardized, each of which is clearly recognizable (over 70%), unblended with other emotions and located on a scale of intensity of expression. Two photographs (one of each sex) of six emotions (happy, sad, fear, anger, surprise and disgust) were selected from each set. In this way altogether 36 (6 emotions×2 sexes×3 cultures) such photographs were selected for the present study.

Preparation of Facial Composites

For the purpose of experimental manipulation the selected photographs were prepared in the form of hemifacial composites and hemiregional composites. In order to prepare hemifacial and hemiregional composites, each selected photograph was printed twice in normal orientation (RL) and twice in mirror reversed orientation (LR). The size of each photograph was 12.5 × 8.5 cm.

Hemifacial Composites

Hemifacial composite may be defined as a lateral half face and its mirror image. For the experimental purposes two types of hemifacial composites i.e. left-left (LL) and right-right (RR) were prepared. These facial composites were prepared by cutting the normal orientation (RL) and its mirror image (LR) orientation of each selected photograph along with its vertical midline. Vertical midline was determined by the internal canthi of the eyes and the central vertex of the upper lip (Rhodes and Lynskey, 1989). After cutting the four prints—two in normal orientation (RL) and two in mirror reversed orientation (LR) of each photograph. A left-left (LL) hemifacial composite was prepared by combining the left hemiface of normal orientation and its mirror image. Similarly, a right-right (RR) facial composite was prepared by combining the right hemiface of normal orientation and its mirror image. In the same way, a pair of left-left (LL) and right-right (RR) facial composites were obtained for each selected photograph.

In order to prepare hemiregional facial composites, a facial composite was selected from each pair of hemifacial composites. The selected hemifacial composites were then cut along the horizontal midline bisecting the upper (forehead, eyebrows, eyes and root of the nose) and lower (lower part of the nose, cheeks, mouth and chin) regions of the face. (Asthana and Mandal,

1997). The lower part of the left-left facial composite was then combined with the upper part the right-right facial composite to have RR/LL hemiregional composite and *vice versa* to get LL/RR.

Altogether six (RL, LR, RR, LL, RR/LL and LL/RR) experimentally manipulated photographs were prepared for each selected photograph giving a total of (36×6) 216 photographs.

Procedure

The six facial photographs (RL, LR, RR, LL, RR/LL, and LL/RR) were ordered in a Latin square arrangement and presented simultaneously. Participants were instructed to scan all the photographs as a whole before making comparison, and they ranked them in terms of intensity of expressed emotion. The most intense expression was to be ranked 1 and the least 6. All 36 sets of photographs were presented to the participants, one set at a time and their responses were recorded on a response sheet.

Statistical Analysis

First of all rank scores of each subject were transferred in the Master Chart and then entered in the SPSS data editor. Then entered data were analysed with the help of statistical computer software SPSS(PC^+) 12.01 version.

Results

The average rank values were computed and analysed with a 3 (Culture: Indian, American, Japanese) × 2 (Sex: male, female)

×3 [Emotion: Positive (Happy, Surprise), Negative aroused (Fear, Anger), Negative non-aroused (Sad, Disgust)] × 6 (Facial Composite: RL, LR, RR, LL, RR/LL, LL/RR) multivariate analysis of variance with repeated measures on all the four factors.

The main effects of culture of expressor, sex of expressor and emotion are not being explained because of the design of the study. Theoretically it was not possible to examine such main effects.

The main effect of facial composite ($F(5,620) = 177.69$, $p<.001$) was statistically significant. The mean values of the six facial composites are shown in Table 1.

Table 1: Mean* (Std Error) Rank of Judgment of Intensity of Expression of Emotion of Six Facial Composites

Facial Composite	*Mean Score*
RL	4.69 (.117)
LR	3.57 (.081)
RR	3.63 (.152)
LL	3.28 (.066)
RR/LL	2.29 (.119)
LL/RR	3.50 (.078)

*Higher the mean score lesser the intensity.

Post-hoc analysis revealed that the RR/LL hemiregional facial composite was judged as most expressive followed by the left-left (LL) facial composite which in turn was judged as significantly more expressive than the other facial presentation ($p<.001$).

The two way interaction effect: Culture × Facial Composite [$F(10,1024) = 1.148$, $p>.05$]; Sex of expressor × Facial

Composite [F(5,620)=.404, p>.05]; Emotion × Facial Composite [F (10,1240)] were not significant.

A four way interaction of Culture × Sex of expressor × Emotion × Facial Composite [F (20, 2480) = 1.59, p<.04] was significant and present a complex pattern of result.

Experiment 2

The findings of the Experiment I suggest that intrahemispheric difference during expression of posed facial expression of emotion. But due to rank-order method, which was used in the Experiment 1 it was not possible to examine many other main effects and interaction effects. Therefore, the second experiment was conducted to examine the phenomenon of facial asymmetry in expression of facial emotion with respect to the sex of expressors, types of emotion, culture of the expressors as well as with different types of facial composites.

METHODOLOGY

Subject

Altogether 125 subjects between the age of 20 to 40 years were participated in the experiment. Subjects were the same who participated in the Experiment 1. Detailed description of the subjects have already been given in Experiment 1.

Tool

Altogether six (RL, LR, RR, LL, RR/LL and LL/RR) experimentally manipulated photographs were prepared for each of six (Happy, sad, fear, agree, surprise and disgust) fundamental emotion for the expressors of three (Indian, American and Japanese) different cultures. In this way total of 216 [6 (Emotion) × 2 (Sexes) × 3 (Culture) × 6 (Composite) photographs were used in the Experiment 2. Details of the photographs development have already been described in the Experiment 1.

Procedure

The six facial photographs (RL, LR, RR, LL, RR/LL and LL/RR) were ordered in a Latin Square arrangement and presented one at a time (successive presentation) to the participants for a period of about 10 second and were asked to judge the intensity of expressed emotion on a 7 point rating scale with 1 being the least intense and 7 being the most intense. Photographs within a set were randomized and presented in a pre-experimentally determined manner. In this way all 216 photographs were presented one by one and subject's responses were recorded on the response sheets.

Statistical Analysis

First of all rating scores of each subject were transferred in the Master chart and then entered in the SPSS Date Editor. Finally, the entered data were analyzed with the help of Statistical software—SPSS (PC+) 12.01 version.

Results

The average rating scores were computed and analyzed with a 3 (Culture: Indian, American, Japanese) × 2 (Sex: Male, female) × 3 (Emotion: Positive (happy, surprise); Negative aroused (fear, anger), and Negatively—Non-aroused (Sad, disgust) × 6 (Facial composite: RL, LR, RR, LL, RR/LL, LL/RR) multivariate analysis of variance with repeated measures on all the four factors. Summary of multivariate analysis of variance are given in Table 2.

Table 2: Summary of 3 (Culture) × 2 (Sex) × 3 (Emotion) × 6 (Facial Composite) Multivariate ANOVA for Rating of Intensity of Expressed Emotion

Source of Variation	*Sum of Squares*	*df*	*Mean Sum of Squares*	*F Value*	*Significance*
Culture of Expressor Error (Culture)	1293.19 870.56	2 248	646.59 3.51	184.21	0.0001
Sex of Expressor Error (Sex)	392.95 495.71	1 124	392.95 3.99	98.31	0.0001
Emotion Error (Emotion)	39.05 764.09	2 248	19.5 3.08	6.33	0.002
Facial composite Error (Facial composite)	25327.47 30683.89	5 620	5065.49 49.48	102.36	0.0001
Culture X Sex Error (Cul. X Sex)	38.12 1001.26	2 248	19.06 4.03	4.72	0.0001
Expressor X Emotion Error (Exp. X Emotion)	804.56 1433.56	4 496	201.14 2.89	69.6	0.0001
Sex X Emotion Error (Sex X Emotion)	325.26 665.74	2 248	162.63 2.68	60.59	0.0001
Culture of Exp. X Sex X Emotion Error (Culture of Exp. X Sex X Emotion)	653.41 1254.86	4 496	163.35 2.59	64.59	0.0001
Expressor X Facial composite Error (Culture of Exp. X Facial composite)	265.72 4774.73	10 1240	26.57 3.85	6.9	0.0001

(Contd.)

(*Contd.*)

Source of Variation	*Sum of Squares*	*df*	*Mean Sum of Squares*	*F Value*	*Sign-ificance*
Sex X Facial composite Error (Sex X Facial composite)	23.76 2078.9	5 620	4.75 3.353	1.41	0.22
Expressor Sex X Facial composite Error (Exp.X Sex X Facial composite)	99.95 4385.32	10 1240	9.99 3.45	2.89	0.002
Emotion X Facial composite Error (Emotion X Facial composite)	175.41 4332.66	10 1240	17.54 3.49	5.02	.0001
Expressor X Emotion X Facial composite Error (Expressor X Emotion X Facial composite)	322.08 8248.31	20 2480	16.1 3.32	4.83	.0001
Sex X Emotion X Facial composite Error (Sex X Emotion X Facial composite)	49.65 3987	10 1240	4.96 3.21	1.54	.122
Expressor X Sex X Emotion X Facial composite Error (Expressor X Sex X Emotion X Facial composite)	257.66 8179	20 2460	12.88 3.32	3.87	.05

The main effect of Culture of expressor [F (2,248) = 184.21, p<.0001], Sex of expressor [F (1,124) = 98.31, p<.0001], Types of emotion [F (2, 248) = 6.337, p<.002] and Facial composite [F (5, 620) = 102.358, p <.0001] were significant.

The significant main effect of culture of the expressor suggested that American expressors (M = 4.60) were judged as expressing emotion significantly more intensely than the Indian expressor (M=4.394), who in turn, were judged more intensely than Japanese expressor (M = 4.22; t = 4.03).

The main effect of sex of expressor revealed that male expressors (M=4.492) were judged as expressing emotion significantly more intensely than the female expressor.

The significant main effect of emotion suggested that positive emotion (M=4.44) were Judged significantly more intense in their expression than the negative aroused (M=4.388) and negatively non-aroused (M=4.386).

The significant main effect of facial composite revealed that RR/LL hemiregional facial composite was judged as expressing emotion more intensely than the left-left (LL) facial composite which in turn was judged as significantly more expressive ($p<.001$) than other facial composite (see Table 3). The present finding corroborates the finding of the Experiment. 1.

Table 3: Mean Rating (Std. Error) of Facial Composites for Intensity of Expressed Emotion

Facial Composite	*Mean Score*
RL	3.53 (.102)
LR	4.43 (.061)
RR	3.98 (.206)
LL	4.77 (.184)
RR/LL	5.79 (.051)
LL/RR	4.35 (.192)

Higher the Mean Greater the Intensity.

The following two way interaction effects were significant: (1) Culture of expressor × Sex of expressor [$F (2, 248) = 4.721$, $p <.01$]; (2) Culture of expressor × Type of emotion [$F (4.496) = 69.95$, $p<.0001$]; (3) Sex of expressor × Type of emotion [$F (2, 248) = 60.59$, $p<.0001$]; (4) Culture of expressor × Facial composite [$F(10, 1240) = 6.90, p < .0001$], (5) Type of emotion × Facial composite [$F(10,1240) = 5.02, p < .0001$].

The significant interaction of Culture × Sex of expressor suggests that Indian and Japanese male expressors were judged as expressing significantly more intensely than their female expressors. Whereas American expressors did not differ from each other (See Table 4).

Table 4: Mean (Std. Error) Rating of Culture of Experssor X Sex of the Expressor for the Judgment of Intensity of Expressed Emotion

Sex	*Culture of Expressor*		
	Indian	*American*	*Japanese*
Male	4.50 (.004)	4.69 (.060)	4.33 (.061)
Female	4.29 (.074)	4.55 (.064)	4.11 (.075)

Higher the mean score greater the intensity.

The interaction of Culture × Emotion was significant. Planned comparison showed that negative aroused and negative non-aroused emotions were judged significantly more expressive in the American expressors followed by Indian expressors and least intensely for Japanese expressors. On the one hand the expressors of these three cultural groups did not differ from each other in terms of intensity of expressed positive emotion (See Table 5).

A significant interaction of Sex of expressor × Emotion revealed that male expressors were judged significantly more expressive than female expressor for positive emotions only. They did not differ from each other for negative aroused and negative non-aroused emotions (See Table 6).

Experiment 2

Table 5: Mean Rating (Std. Error) of Expresssor X Emotion for the judgment of Intensity of Expressed Facial Emotion

	Culture of Expressor		
Emotion	*Indian*	*American*	*Japanese*
Positive	4.41 (.072)	4.42 (.070)	4.46 (.074)
Negative Aroused	4.38 (.078)	4.69 (0.65)	4.08 (.062)
Negative Non-aroused	4.37 (.066)	4.68 (.066)	4.10 (0.75)

Higher the mean score greater the intensity.

Table 6: Mean Rating (Std. Error) of Sex of the Experssor X Emotion for the Judgment of Intensity of Expressed Facial Emotion

	Sex of Expressor	
Emotion	*Male*	*Female*
Positive	4.63 (.058)	4.25 (.079)
Negative Aroused	4.45 (.060)	4.32 (.060)
Negative Non-aroused	4.33 (.056)	4.38 (.072)

The interaction of culture × facial composite was also significant. It suggests that subjects' judgment for expressors of three cultural groups did not differ regarding RR/LL and LL facial composite. On the other hand, RL, LR and RR facial composites were judged significantly more expressive for American expressors than the Japanese expressors. Although, Indian expressors and Japanese expressors did not differ from each other on those facial composite (See Table 7).

Table 7: Mean Rating (Std. Error) of Culture of Expressor X Facial Composite for Judgment of Intensity of Expressed Facial Emotion

	Culture of Expressor		
Facial Composite	*Indian*	*American*	*Japanese*
RL	3.42 (.111)	3.81 (.112)	3.31 (.126)
LR	4.42 (.09)	4.63 (.08)	4.23 (.085)
RR	4.02 (.229)	4.27 (.215)	3.66 (.204)
LL	4.57 (.20)	4.73 (.166)	4.42 (.191)
RR/LL	5.82 (.076)	5.81 (.073)	5.61 (.061)
LL/RR	4.11 (.202)	4.31 (.199)	4.05 (.207)

There are many other three ways significant interaction effect. These are:

(1) Culture × Sex of expressor × Emotion [$F(4,496)= 64.59$ $p<.0001$]. The three ways interaction indicated that positive emotions were judged significantly more expressive in males than in females of Indian and Japanese expressors but not for American expressors. It suggest that American females were most expressive in negative aroused emotion than Indian and Japanese female expressors. Negative non-aroused emotions were judged significantly more expressive in Indian female expressor, whereas the trend was reversed for Americans (See Table 8).

(2) A significant Culture × Sex of expressor × Facial composite suggests that Indian and Japanese male expressors were judged more expressive than female

expressors on almost all facial representations. On the other hand, American male and female expressors were judged almost equally in intensity of expressed emotion, on most of the facial composite except one i.e. LL/RE (See Table 9).

Table 8: Mean Rating (Std. Error) of Culture of Expresssor X Sex of Expressor X Emotion for the Judgment of Intensity of Expressed Facial Emotion

Emotion	*Culture of Expressor*					
	Indian		*American*		*Japanese*	
	Male	*Female*	*Male*	*Female*	*Male*	*Female*
Positive	4.83 (.071)	4.04 (.102)	4.41 (.080)	4.43 (.085)	4.65 (.077)	4.28 (.095)
Negative Aroused	4.44 (.093)	4.33 (.087)	4.73 (.081)	4.70 (.076)	4.19 (.076)	3.97 (.037)
Negative Non-aroused	4.23 (.082)	4.50 (.078)	4.79 (.068)	4.57 (.087)	4.12 (.078)	4.08 (.098)

Table 9: Mean Rating (Std. Error) of Culture of Experssor X Sex of Expressor X Facial Composite for the Judgment of Intensity of Expressed Emotion

Facial Composite	*Indian*		*American*		*Japanese*	
	Male	*Female*	*Male*	*Female*	*Male*	*Female*
RL	3.57 (.125)	3.27 (.134)	3.87 (.118)	3.80 (.140)	3.38 (.153)	3.26 (.130)
LR	4.54 (.127)	4.30 (.103)	4.70 (.090)	4.56 (.100)	4.35 (.105)	4.10 (.106)
RR	4.13 (.235)	3.91 (.254)	4.31 (.231)	4.24 (.222)	3.8 (.200)	3.76 (.232)
LL	4.66 (.208)	4.50 (.212)	4.74 (.178)	4.73 (.217)	4.69 (.990)	4.23 (.200)
RR/LL	5.93 (.087)	5.71 (.100)	5.81 (.094)	5.81 (.093)	5.62 (.079)	5.60 (.100)
LL/RR	4.16 (.186)	4.06 (.252)	4.46 (.191)	4.16 (.236)	4.16 (.215)	3.94 (.218)

Experiment 3

Although, Experiment 2 was primarily intended to examine the effects of sex of expressor, types of emotion and culture of the expressor on phenomenon of facial asymmetry during expression of emotion. Such effects have been reflected in the results of Experiment 2 also. The present experiment was mainly conducted to examine the role of cultural display rules in facial asymmetry during expression of facial emotion. Sex of expressor and categories of emotions were also taken into consideration to substantiate the results of the Experiment 2 with methodological refinement.

METHODOLOGY

Subjects

Altogether seventy subjects between the ages of 20 to 40 years were selected from the different regions of Uttarakhand for participation in the present experiment. Since handedness is considered as one of the important factor to influence neuropsychological researches, the hand preference of each subject was assessed by using the Hand Preference Schedule developed by Mandal, Pandey, Singh and Asthana (1992). Subjects with a hand preference quotient below +.25 were not included in the study sample (range: left always –1.00 to right always +1.00). Therefore, all participants were clearly right-handed.

Subjects with a history of hand change were not considered. Information regarding familial handedness was also obtained. Subjects with (i) impaired sighting performance, and (ii) history of brain disease were also excluded from the study.

Tool

Three standardized sets of photographs depicting six fundamental emotions (Happy, Sad, Fear, Anger, Surprise, and Disgust) were used in the present experiment. These three sets of photographs were the (1) Picture of Facial Affect developed by Mandal (1987) based on Indian Expressors, (2) Ekman and Friesen (1987) with American Expressors, and (3) Mandal, Harizuka, Bhushan and Mishra (2001) with Japanese Expressors. The standardization process of the photographs has already been described in the Experiment 1.

Two photographs (one of each sex) of six emotions (Happy, Sad, Fear, Anger, Surprise, and Disgust) were selected from each set. In this way altogether, 36 [6 (Emotions) × 2 (Sex) × 3 (Cultures)]. Such Photographs were selected for the present experiment.

For the purpose of experimental manipulation, the left-left (LL) and the right-right (RR) facial composites were prepared. In order to prepare hemifacial composite photograph, each selected photograph was printed twice—one in normal orientation (RL) and the other in mirror-reversed orientation (LR). The facial composites were prepared by cutting the normal orientation (RL) and its mirror image (LR) orientation of each selected photograph along with the vertical midline. The vertical midline was determined by the internal canthi of the eyes and the central vertex of the upper lip (Rhodes and Lynskey, 1989). After cutting both the prints of each selected photographs, a LL (left-left) composite was prepared by combining the left hemiface of normal orientation and its mirror image. Similarly, a right-right (RR) facial composite was prepared by joining the right hemiface of normal orientation (RL) and its mirror image (LR). In this way, altogether 108 photographs (36 different sets of three facial orientations)—RL, LL, and RR were used in the present experiment.

Procedure

In this experiment a set of photographs comprised identical facial orientation of three different cultures depicting similar emotion by same sex of expressors. Put in other words, for example, a set may be a RL orientation of Indian, American and Japanese male expressors depicting happy emotion. In this way, 36 different sets were there.

In this experiment, paired comparison method was utilized for the presentation of the stimuli. Therefore, a set of three photographs were combined in all possible pairs within the set. In this way, there were 3 different pairs for each set. The sequences of pairs were determined pre-experimentally and each photograph appeared equally often on the right and on the left to control the effect of hemispatial bias. With this arrangement, a pair of photographs was presented to the subjects and they were asked to prefer one that looked more expressive and to show no preference if they find no difference in expressivity.

Statistical Analysis

First of all total number of preferences for each member of the paired photographs were calculated for each subject separately. Then the preference scores were transferred in the Master Chart to enter the data in the SPSS data editor. Finally, the entered data were statistically analysed with the help of a statistical computer software—SPSS (PC) 12.01 version.

Results

The mean of preference scores were obtained and analysed with a 3 (Facial Composites: RL, LL, RR) × 3 (Emotions: Positive (Happy, Surprise), Negatively aroused (Fear, Anger); Negatively non-aroused (Sad, Disgust)) ×2 (Sex: male, female) × 3 (Cultures: Indian, American, Japanese) multivariate analysis of variance with repeated measures on all factors.

Due to the design of the experiment, the main effect of Facial Composites, types of emotions and sex of the expressor could not be examined. There are two emotions in each category that is why maximum mean of preference would be 6.

The main effect of Culture of expressor [$F (2,138) = 39.23$, $p < .0001$] was significant. The main effect of culture of expressor suggested that Japanese expressors (M=1.43) were significantly least preferred than the Americans (M=2.26) and Indian expressors (M=2.302) in terms of intensity of its expressions.

The interaction of Sex of expressor × Culture of expressor ($F (2,138)=4.83$, $p < .01$) was significant. It suggests that Indian male expressors (M=2.359) were significantly more preferred than American male expressors (M=2.17) in terms of its intensity of expression while female expressors the trend was reversed (See Table 10).

Table 10: Mean Preference (Std. Error) of Culture of Experssor X Sex of Experssor for Photographs Depicting Facial Emotion

Sex	*Indian*	*American*	*Japanese*
Male	2.36 (.073)	2.17 (.055)	1.48 (.073)
Female	2.24 (.073)	2.35 (.072)	1.40 (.073)

Higher the mean greater the preference.

The interaction of Facial composites × Emotions [F(4,276)=2.513], p <.04, See Table 11) and Facial composites × Culture of Expressors [F(4,276)= 2.319, p<.05, See Table 12] were also significant but need not to explain because of Four ways interaction of Facial Composite × Emotion × Sex of expressor × Culture of expressor [F(8,552) = 6.752, p <.001, See Table 13] was significant.

Table 11: Mean Preference (Std. Error) of Facial Composite X Emotion for Photographs Depicting Facial Emotion

Facial Composite	*Positive*	*Negative Aroused*	*Negative Non-Aroused*
LR	2.01 (.006)	2.00 (.002)	1.99 (.005)
LL	2.00 (.002)	1.99 (.007)	1.99 (.002)
RR	1.99 (.002)	1.99 (.002)	2.00 (.002)

Table 12: Mean Preference (Std. Error) of Facial Composite X Culture of Expressor for Photograph Depicting Facial Emotion

Facial composite	*Culture of Expressor*		
	Indian	*American*	*Japanese*
RL	2.374 (.078)	2.23 (.074)	1.39 (.088)
LL	2.23 (.079)	2.23 (.064)	1.52 (.078)
RR	2.30 (.071)	2.31 (.062)	1.38 (.060)

Table 13: Mean Preference (Std. Error) of Facial Composite X Emotion X Sex of Expressor X Culture of Expressor for Photograph Depicting Facial Emotion

Sex	*Emotion**								
	Positive			*Negative aroused*			*Negative non-aroused*		
	Indian	*American*	*Japanese*	*Indian*	*American*	*Japanese*	*Indian*	*American*	*Japanese*
Male	2.75 (.0870)	1.97 (.115)	1.30 (.100)	223 (.143)	2.08 (.118)	1.70 (.134)	2.42 (.121)	2.28 (.112)	1.29 (.129)
RL Female	2.27 (.125)	2.35 (.113)	1.40 (.107)	2.37 (.119)	2.37 (.129)	1.25 (.134)	2.18 (.117)	2.33 (.116)	1.44 (.125)
Male	2.43 (.114)	(.085) 2.11	1.47 (.116)	2.09 (.109)	2.14 (.106)	1.77 (.127)	2.24 (.126)	2.19 (.120)	1.69 (.121)
LL Female	2.23 (.117)	2.14 (.111)	1.56 (.118)	2.20 (.116)	2.45 (.099)	1.28 (.126)	2.20 (.116)	2.33 (.127)	1.46 (.133)
Male	2.15 (.136)	2.15 (.120)	1.69 (.121)	2.24 (.129)	2.56 (.107)	1.20 (.095)	2.66 (.127)	2.10 (.117)	1.26 (.120)
RR Female	2.47 (.123)	2.47 (.123)	2.46 (.127)	1.06 (.109)	2.33 (.101)	1.57 (.134)	2.19 (.1260)	2.29 (.115)	1.53 (.105)

* There are two emotions in each category. That is why altogether 6 different pairs of preferences for each category of emotion.

It suggests that positive emotions were significantly more pronounced in the right hemiface of Japanese male expressor and Indian female expressor than the other two cultural groups of their own sex. When mean preference scores of right-right and left-left facial composite for negative aroused emotions were compared, a significant difference was found for American male expressors as well as for Japanese expressors. It suggested that American male expressors were judged as significantly more expressive in RR orientation followed by Indian male expressors and least expressed by Japanese male expressors. Japanese expressors were judged as significantly least intense in negatively aroused emotion in RR orientation. Remaining other differences could not reach up to the level of significance.

Regarding negatively non-aroused emotion, it was found that Japanese male and female expressors were judged as expressing significantly less intensely negative non-aroused emotion on right facial composite than the Indian and American expressors.

General Discussion

The first two alternative hypotheses of the study that "the hemiregional facial composite involving upper right-right and lower left-left part (RR/LL) would be most expressive in terms of expression of emotion than any other hemiregional and hemifacial composite" and "a left hemiface would be more expressive than right hemiface in expression of emotion" have been supported by the results of the Experiment 1 and Experiment 2.

The findings show that hemiregional composites of facial expression involving RR/LL were judged as the most expressive followed by left facial composite, irrespective of sex, emotion and culture of the expressor. It substantiates the findings of the earlier study in which the proposition was originally put forward (Asthana and Mandal, 1997), that upper and lower part of hemifaces are differentially involved during expression of facial emotion. Although the greater left hemifacial activity has been supported in several other studies (Asthana and Mandal, 1998; Borod, 1993; Campbell, 1986; see review by Asthana, Bhushan and Mandal, 2000; Mandal, Asthana and Biswal, 2008; Skinner and Mullen, 1991; Borod, Haywood and Koff, 1997).

Neuroanatomical researches suggest that facial muscles especially in the lower region are contralaterally innervated by the fibre projections of the two cerebral hemispheres (Borod and Koff, 1984). Since the right hemisphere mediates the function of emotional processing, the left hemiface is found in general to be more expressive. These results, however cannot fully account for the present findings in which the left hemifacial involvement was specific to the lower facial region and the upper region showed a right hemifacial involvement during emotion expression (Borod and Koff, 1990) and second, upper region of the left hemiface was judged as less expressive because the hemifacial sides of that region expressive in a different way from the hemifacial sides of the lower region. The first possibility suggests that the left half of face was judged as more expressive because of its voluntary control over the small muscles in the lower region. The upper part was either redundant or functionally/motorically less active. The lesser degree of motoric activity during posed expression may be attributed to less voluntary muscle control of the upper region, including eye brows, and corners of the eyes (Rinn, 1984). Although less prominent than the lower face, the facial action present in the upper region during posed expression may also neutralize the emotion effect (functional redundancy) due to its differential innervation from the right hemisphere. It is possible that facial nerves originating in the right hemisphere are distributed uncrossed to the upper region of the face. Therefore, the side of the upper face ipsilateral to the right hemisphere will be relatively more expressive than the side contralateral to the right hemisphere. In the case of the predominant bilateral fibre projections to the facial muscles, there would be no facial asymmetry in the upper region. Borod and Koff (1984) also noted that a unilateral cortical lesion of the face area does not invariably produced paralysis or weakness in the contralateral hemiface. Such an observation implies that there may also be some ipsilateral innervation (p. 28).

Considered together, the results suggest that expression of emotion in the upper region of the face might be controlled ipsilaterally rather than contralaterally and support the earlier hypothesis that right hemisphere is relatively dominant in the expression of emotion.

The present finding suggests that overall male expressors were judged as more expressive than female expressors. Sex difference in expressiveness of facial emotion suggests that expression of emotion is more strongly lateralized in males than females. Smith (2000) also found that the direction of these asymmetries differed in males and females. Males had significantly more left facedness than females. Smith interpreted the finding as being caused by brain's hemispheres having different levels of involvement in males and females in certain types of thinking. For example studies have suggested that an average female performs better than males on tasks predominantly controlled by the left hemisphere such as verbal tasks (Graves, Goodglass and Landars, 1982; Hausman, Behrendtkorbitz, Kantz, Lamm, Radelt and Gunturkun, 1998; Loring, Meador, Allesion and Wright, 2000) and males performed better on tasks predominantly controlled by right hemisphere (Voyer, 1996).

According to Smith (2000) cognitive tasks that involve one hemisphere more than the other may result in greater muscle size on the side of the face controlled by that hemisphere. Smith suggests that because on an average, females and males rely on verbal and visuospatial thinking to different extents; this affects the facial musculature of males and females. As a result males tend to have larger left face which is under the control of right hemisphere and females tend to have a larger right face which is controlled by the left hemisphere (Smith,

2000). This was supported through earlier work on facial asymmetry and facial muscle activity (Smith, Smith and Smith, 1991) suggesting that hemiface size may be influenced by muscular activity. Keles *et al.* (1997) also reported that males had a significant larger left hemiface while females showed no clear differences.

Significant differences between the ratings of male and female expressors may also be because of specific characteristics of these two groups. The females because of gender role expectations were rated as less expressive than males. On the other hand, other studies using a variety of different techniques to measure facial asymmetry have failed to find a relationship between gender and facial asymmetry (Borod, Haywood and Koff, 1997; Borod, Koff, Yecer, Santsche and Schmidt, 1998).

The major finding of the study was the significant culture effect suggesting cultural influences on expressions of emotion. American expressors were judged as most expressive followed by Indian and Japanese expressors. Some studies have also documented cultural differences as a function of the judged intensity of expressed emotion (e.g. Ekman *et al.*, 1987; Mandal, Bryden, Bulman-Flemming, 1996).

Mastumoto (1989) argued that although emotions are biologically programmed process of learning to control both their expression and perception largely dependent on cultural factors. Russel (1994) suggested that specific emotional categories are largely culturally specific. Elferbein and Ambady (2002, 2003) have reported that countries with higher scores on individualism show higher level of general emotional expressions. More expressions may be expected for countries scoring high on the autonomy factor. Americans would be certainly high on autonomy factor than the Indian and Japanese. Secondly, Americans belong to individualistic society whereas Indian and Japanese belong to collective societies.

It seems that societies imposing fewer restrictions on behaviour and with less strict social norms report emotions more freely. This is in line with the concept of tightness (Pelto, 1968; Triandis, 1990 b; Triandis and Suh, 2002). In loose cultures, norms are imposed strictly and deviation from norms is less frowned upon possibly also resulting in a higher level of emotional expression.

A significant interaction of Culture × Emotion revealed that negative emotion expressions were more expressive in American followed by Indian and Japanese expressors whereas for positive emotions no difference was found. Earlier studies also pointed out that Japanese expressors tend to mask their negative affect expression (Friesen, 1972). The negative emotional expressions are less distinctively identifiable in Indians as compared to North American participants has also been in evidence (Mandal, Bryden and Bulman-Flemming, 1996). The present findings lend support to this observation, suggesting that while Japanese expressors tend to mask, Indians tend to neutralize their negative feelings as compared to American expressors.

Hofstede (2001) noted that in individualist societies, the expression of happiness is encouraged at the cost of expression of sadness while this is reversed in collectivist societies. Much research has focused on the individualism-collectivism dimension or the related distinction between independence-interdependence of the self (e.g. Markus and Kitayema,1991; Triandis, 1990 a, 1995). Extensive theoretical arguments and empirical evidence have been presented suggesting relationship between the syndrome and emotional expression (Greenfield, 1994; Kagitcibasi, 1996; Kitayema, Markus, and Matsumoto, 1995; Mesquita, 2001; Oyserman, Coon and Kemmelmer, 2002).

There were many three ways interaction effects which were also significant. The significant interaction of Culture × Sex of expressor × Emotion revealed that positive emotions were judged more expressive in Indian and Japanese male expressors than their female expressors. American females were most expressive than their Indian and Japanese counterparts in negative aroused emotion whereas Indian females were most expressive for negative non-aroused emotion.

These findings suggest a sex specific social learning for these cultures. In fact, traditional societies (as in India and Japan) are male dominated and there is likelihood that the expression used for the facility of social interaction is communicated with greater intensity. Americans were unaffected by sex specific vocabulary in facial expressions.

There was a significant four ways interaction of Facia' composite × Emotion × Sex of expressor × Culture. It suggests that positive emotions were significantly more pronounced in the right-face than the left hemiface of Japanese male expressors whereas similar trend was with Indian female expressors. Regarding negatively aroused emotions, it was most expressive in the right-hemiface of American male expressors followed by Indian male expressors and least expressed by Japanese male expressors for negatively non-aroused emotions. Japanese male and female expressors were judged as least expressive on their right hemiface, followed by Indian and American expressors.

These findings partially substantiate the neurocultural theory of Ekman (1994). He proposed that basic emotions are stored in an innate facial affect programme and cultural display rules alter these expressions in accordance with the social context. It is now established that facial behaviour during emotional stimulation is affected by the social context in which such stimulation occurs (Fridlund, 1991, 1994; Hess, Banse, and Kappers, 1995; Jakobs, Manstead and Fischer, 1999a, 1999b). For example, compared to an 'alone' condition, the presence of other persons engaging in the same tasks influence participants' facial behaviour during emotional stimulation. It is widely assumed explanation that we have learned through a process of socialization to exercise to control over facial behaviour (Garner, 1996; Zeman and Garber, 1996). Ekman and Friesen (1969) were the first investigators to provide a clear definition of such display rules. In a subsequent publication they wrote: "We have coined the phrase display rules to describe what people learn, probably quite early in their lives, about the need to manage the appearance of particular emotions in particular situations" (Ekman and Friesen, 1975, p. 137). They have described the six possible ways in which display rules can affect facial behaviour:

(1) People can facilitate or inhibit their facial behaviour.
(2) Extreme inhibition is termed as neutralization.
(3) Not showing a felt emotion but instead of replacing it with an unfelt emotion is called masking.
(4) Responding with one's face despite the fact that no emotion is felt is called simulation.
(5) Adding an expression as a comment on an emotion you must have shown is called qualifying.
(6) Culture display rules motivate people to act prosocially (i.e. to protect the feelings of others).

More recently, Reissland and Harris (1991) have provided a description of the prerequisites for using display rules (based on Snyder, 1974) "display rules require the motivation and ability to control one's behaviour in accordance with one's knowledge of the appropriateness of a particular emotional expression in a particular context" (p. 43). This may be the reason why American males were judged as more expressive than the Indian and Japanese expressors in negative aroused and negative non-aroused emotion in their right hemiface. While Japanese and Indians were more expressive, especially Japanese males and Indian female expressors in expressing positive emotion on the right face i.e. the social face.

Wolff (1933) observed that the right side of the face offers social and public expressions, whereas the left side of the face reveals hidden, personalized feelings. Because the right side of the face is the public side, conscious control of it is rendered in terms of social display norms for expression of emotion such as intensification, deintensification, neutralization and masking (Ekman, 1982). In day-to-day interaction, emotions are expressed normally through left hemiface (a function of the right hemisphere) and the cognitive control of the right hemiface (a function of the left hemisphere) is rendered by the display norm of either disintensification or neutralization.

Men's display of anger has been reported to be both more pervasive and is generally more acceptable (see Brody and Hall, 2000; Fischer, 1993). Ekman and Friesen (1973) found that both American and Japanese students who watched stress films showed the same facial expression when they were alone. When they answered questions about new stress films in the presence of others, however, the Japanese subjects inhibited their negative facial expression and simulated positive ones.

In a study Kowner and Ogawa (1993) reported that a traditional gender role expectation that is present in Japan is that women are expected to exhibit servile manners and to show compassion towards others. Therefore, it is possible that Japanese female expressors were least expressive in expression of negative emotions than any other cultural group. Lebra (1976) indicated that for Japanese, facial expressions of displeasure are replaced by the expression of smiling, which helps them to focus on interaction without their attention being drawn towards the source of annoyance. Such cognitive strategy underlying the display of emotion may also alter the intensity of expressed emotion. Possibly the positive emotions are learned to be displayed more intensely by the side of the face which is more under the voluntary control—the right face: (see Asthana and Mandal, 1996) for the facility of social interaction in Japan.

There was a significant interaction of sex with culture and emotion. It was found that happiness was judged to have been expressed more intensely in males than in females for Indian and Japanese expressors. This finding suggests a sex specific social learning for collectivistic societies (such as in India and Japan) are male dominated and there is greater likelihood that the expression used for the facility of social interaction, the expression of happiness is conveyed with greater intensity. Americans were not affected by sex specific variability especially in positive emotions.

On the other hand, it was found that negative emotions (i.e. especially, negatively aroused) have more pronounced in the right face of American male expressors followed by Indian and least intense by Japanese male expressors. With regard to emotional responses many studies indicate that basic emotions such as sadness, fear and anger are universally experienced (e.g. Ekman and Friesen, 1971; Izard, 1971; Wallbott and Scherer, 1988). However, some studies suggest that frequency or intensity of these emotions may vary with culture (Babad and Wallbott 1986; Matsumoto, 1989; Wallbott and Scherer, 1988), According to appraisal theories, if people from two cultures appraise the same event in the same way, then they should feel the same emotions. But if people from two cultures appraise the same event in different ways, they may feel different emotions or different intensities of emotion. That is cultural differences in appraisal may be able to explain cultural differences in emotion because of underlying cross-culture similarities in appraisal-emotion relationships. Because of cross-cultural similarities in appraisal-emotion relationship, cultural differences in expression of emotion may result. That is differences between Americans and Indians in situational state, motivational state, and probably power may explain differences, in intensity of sadness, fear and anger. Across sadness, fear and anger situations Indians reported lower sadness than Americans and lower anger than Americans (Roseman, 1995). That is, Indians' tendency to see event more motive consistent may account for their lower intensity of negative emotions.

Another possibility is that Indians are influenced by different culturally rooted philosophical orientations to actions and their outcomes than the Americans. The *Bhagavad-Gita* emphasises the importance of detachment. It focuses on action rather than their outcomes. The 'Gita' claims that this orientation to action rather their outcomes diminishes stress (Sharma, 1989) and negative emotions including sadness, fear and anger (Kuppaswamy, in Murphy and Murphy, 1968) and enhances one's capacity for lasting joy.

In contrast, it would seem that deep rooted traditions within American culture place great emphasis on outcomes. For example, the idea that one's moral worth or virtue will be reflected in the outcomes one brings forth is Americans tend to subscribe to a "Just World theory" (Lerner, 1980; Sampson, 1981) in which individuals are presumed to obtain the outcomes they deserve. While middle class Americans also tend to have relatively high expectations for success (see Madsen and Kagan, 1973) define achievement in terms of outcomes (Duda, 1981; cited in Misra and Agarwal, 1985) and evaluate people in terms of their accomplishment (Williams, 1969). One more explanation for cultural differences may be that Indians may perceive negative outcomes as less controllable or modifiable than Americans do (Schuster, *et al.*, 1989), resign themselves more readily to what has happened, and thus perceive less discrepancy from what is desired and feel less negative emotion. Indians might tend to regard outcomes as less modifiable as a result of greater dependence or uncontrollable external events.

Culture, in turn, can affect person's motives. For example, Markus and Kitayama (1991) argue that the central goal in many Western cultures is to attain independence from other individuals. Whereas many non-Western cultures seek to maintain interdependence (Hofstede, 1980; Triandis, 1986) Thus difference in motive can also generate differences in emotion.

It has been argued that display rules may not be the sole source of cultural differences in expression of emotions because the important thing may not be the expression itself, but the rules of conduct and respect in certain interactions (Mesquita, Frijda and Scherer, 1997). As Lebra (1976) indicated that Japanese replaced their facial expression of displeasure by the expression of smile, which helps them to focus on interaction without their attention being drawn towards the source of annoyance. Such cognitive strategy underlying the display of emotions (Akiyama, 1992) may also alter the expression behaviour. It may also be noted that in any collectivistic society as in India (Sinha and Tripathi, 1994;) or Japan (Yamafuchi, 1994) the idea of distributing displeasure is rarely entertained. The present finding subscribes to this viewpoint.

Conclusion

The present findings suggest that although individuals of different cultures express their facial emotion almost in the same way, but socialization pattern of a given culture regulates these expressions. Present findings particularly support the Ekman's neurocultural theory of emotion, "basic emotions are stored in an innate facial affect programme and cultural display rules alter these expressions in accordance with the social context".

In addition to the support of neurocultural theory of emotion, the present findings throw light how neurocultural component interact with hemiface, sex of expressor and valence of emotion. It appears from the finding that emotional valence induced cultural variability. Negative emotions were expressed most intensely by American expressors followed by Indian and then Japanese expressors. It is believed that negative emotions are less often expressed publicly in a collectivistic society (India, Japan) as these expressions are often taken as defiance to social norms (Matsumoto, 1989;1993), Mandal, Bryden and Bulman Flemming (1996) and Mandal, Harizuka, Bhushan and Mishra (2001) also partially support the present finding that Indians have deintensifying fear and anger as compared to Americans. In fact, individuals in a collectivistic society (such as India and Japan) learn to sacrifice the negative emotional reactions in favour of group ideals (Hofsiede,1980). Whereas individualistic society may sanction the communication of these emotions more as they relate to the freedom of the individual to express and perceive negative emotions (Matsumoto, 1989).

One very interesting finding of the present study is that neurocultural component has interaction with facial presentations. These observations substantiate the view that facial expression of emotions are governed both by mechanism associated with facial side (neuro) and by learned display rules (cultural).

Summary of the Finding

The prime objective of the present study was to examine whether culture display rules of three different cultures (i.e. Indian, American, and Japanese) differentially influence to different hemifaces, valence of emotion and sex of expressor during expression of emotion. In addition to this, hemifacial asymmetry and hemiregional asymmetry in expression of emotion among the expressor of these cultures were also examined.

In order to achieve the objectives of the present study, the different hypotheses were formulated and tested empirically. Results of the study can be summarized as given below:

(1) The first two hypotheses of the study were related to the hemiregional and hemifacial asymmetry in expression of emotion. Both the alternative hypotheses were accepted. The findings suggest that hemiregional facial composite involving upper right-right and lower left-left (RR/LL) was most expressive followed by left facial composite than any other facial presentation. It suggests that greater left hemifacial involvement was specific to the lower two-third portion and the upper one-third region showed a greater right hemifacial involvement during emotion expression.

(2) Sex of the expressor was found to be a significant variable in the judgment intensity of expressed

emotion. Overall male expressor, irrespective of any culture, were judged to have expressed emotion more intensely than the female expressor.

(3) The major finding of the study was the significant culture influence on expression of emotion. American expressors were judged as most expressive followed by Indians who in turn, were judged more expressive than Japanese expressors.

(4) Positive emotions (happy and surprise) were found more intensely expressed than negative aroused (fear, anger) and negatively non-aroused (sad and disgust) irrespective of the culture of the expressors.

(5) A significant interaction of culture of the expressor × emotion revealed that negative emotion expressions were judged most expressive in American expressors followed by Indian and least intense by the Japanese expressors. No cultural difference was found for positive emotions.

(6) The significant interaction of culture × sex of the expressor × emotion suggests that positive emotions were found to be more expressive in Indian and Japanese male expressors than their female counterparts. Negative aroused emotions were significantly more intensely expressed by American female expressors than Indian and Japanese females. When the results were analyzed with respect to negative non-aroused emotions, Indian females were found to be most expressive than the expressors of any other culture. These findings suggest a sex specific social learning for these cultures.

(7) A four way interaction of facial composite × emotion × sex of the expressor × culture was also significant. It presents a very complex pattern of result. It suggests that positive emotions were judged as significantly more pronounced on the right hemiface of Japanese male expressors than Indian and American male expressors. Whereas similar trend was found with Indian female expressors. Regarding negatively aroused emotions, it was found that the right hemiface of the American male expressors were judged as most expressive followed by Indian and least expressed by Japanese expressors. For negatively non-aroused emotion Japanese male as well as female expressors were judged significantly least intensely expressed emotion on their right hemiface than the Indians and Americans.

Significance of the Study

The present book is related to cross-cultural neuropsychology of facial emotion. This is an emerging discipline that examines behavioural neuroscience within a cultural context. Very little is known about this area of research, especially in Indian context. Therefore, the present book has significance in the said area of research.

The specific achievement of the present study is that it was well planned, defined and controlled scientific attempt to examine the role of neuro as well as cultural display rules in expression of facial emotion. The finding of the study is in the direction to support the theory. It was found that individuals of different cultures express their facial emotion almost in the same way but socialization pattern of a given culture regulates these expressions, especially the negative emotions. It appears from the finding that emotional valence induced cultural variability. Negative emotions were expressed most intensely by Americans followed by Indians and least by Japanese. It is believed that negative emotions are less often expressed publicly in a collective society (like India and Japan). They learn to scarifice their negative emotional reactions in favour of group ideas. This cultural variability has interacted with hemiface and sex of the expressor.

Another significance of the book is that in the earlier book the present author along with co-author has introduced an innovative facial stimuli i.e. hemiregional facial composite to examine differential role of upper and lower hemifaces in expression of facial emotion. The importance of hemiregional facial composite has already been examined with Indian expressors only. The present findings corroborate the result of earlier studies and suggest that in order to have a better understanding of facial expression of emotion such stimuli can be used across the culture to examine the phenomenon of hemifacial asymmetry in expression of emotion. It will also advance our understanding of both communication and construction of emotion. The present finding may be utilized for emotional deception and interpersonal leakage during face to face interaction.

In general, people are less aware about the fact that two sides of human face are not equally expressive. Present findings empirically support the notion that left hemiface, especially lower two-third part of the face is relatively more expressive than their counterpart. On the basis of the present finding, it may be speculated that we learn in the course of human development to civilize intense emotional expression by the right hemiface which is more under the control of less emotional side of the cerebral hemisphere (i.e. left hemisphere) for the facility of social interaction. In order to develop effective communication skills, an individual may be given training to focus more on expressor's left hemiface because this side reveals expressor's personal and emotional feeling strongly.

References

Akiyama, H. (1992). Measurement of depressive symptoms in cross-cultural research. *Paper presented at the International Conference on Emotion and Culture. University of Oregon, Eugene.*

Asthana, H.S., and Ahmed I. (2005). Intra- and inter-hemifacial asymmetry in expression of emotion: A proposition revisited. *Research Journal of Philosophy and Social Sciences, 31*, 1-10.

Asthana, H.S., Bhushan, B., and Mandal, M.K. (2000). Side bias in facial expression. In M.K. Mandal, M.B. Bulman-Flemming and G. Tiwari (Eds.), *Side bias: A Neuropsychological Perspective* (pp. 289-312). Kulwer Academic Press: The Netherlands.

Asthana, H.S., and Mandal, M.K. (1996). Mirror reversal of a face is perceived as expressing emotion more intensely. *Behavioural Neurology, 9*, 115-117.

———(1997). Hemiregional variations in facial expression of emotion. *British Journal of Psychology, 88*, 519-525.

———(1998). Hemifacial asymmetry in emotion expression. *Behaviour Modification* (*Special Issue: Facial expression of emotions*), *22*, 177-183.

Baribeau, I., Guerettee, R., and Braun, C. (1987). Hemifacial production of posed emotional expression in normal men and women. *Paper presented at the meeting of The International Neuropsychological Society*, Washington, DC.

Borod, J.C. (1992). Interhemispheric and intrahemispheric control of emotion: A focus on unilateral brain damage. *Journal of Consulting and Clinical Psychology, 60*, 339-348.

Borod, J.C. (1993). Cerebral mechanisms underlying facial, prosodic and lexical emotional expression: A review of neuropsychological studies and methodological issues. *Neuropsychology, 7,* 445-463.

Borod, J.C., and Caron, H.S. (1980). Facedness and emotion related to lateral dominance, sex and expression type. *Neuropsychologia, 18,* 237-242.

Borod, J.C., Caron, H.S., and Koff, E. (1981). Asymmetry of facial expression related to handedness, and eyedness: A quantitative study. *Cortex, 17,* 380-390.

Borod, J.C., Koff, E., Yecker, S., Santschi, C., and Schmidt, J.M. (1988). Facial asymmetry during emotional expression: Gender, valence, and measurement technique. *Neuropsychologia, 36,* 1209-1215.

Borod, J.C., Haywood, C.S., and Koff, E. (1997). Neuropsychological aspects of facial asymmetry during emotional expression: A review of the normal adult literature. *Neuropsychology Review, 7,* 41-60.

Borod, J.C., and Koff, E. (1984). Asymmetries in affective expression: behaviour and anatomy. In N. Fox and R. Davidson (Eds.), *The Psychobiology of affective development.* Hillsdale, NJ: Erlbaum.

———(1990). Lateralization for facial emotional behaviour: A methodological perspective. *International Journal of Psychology, 25,* 157-177.

Borod, J.C., Koff, E., and Caron, H.S. (1983). Right hemispheric specialization for the expression of emotion: A focus on the face. In E. Perceman (Ed.), *Cognitive function in the right hemisphere.* New York: Academic Press.

Borod, J.C., Kent, Koff, E., Martin, C., and Alpert, M. (1998). Facial asymmetry while posing positive and negative emotions: Supports for the right hemisphere hypothesis. *Neuropsychologia, 26,* 759-764.

Borod, J.C., St. Clair. J., Koff, E., Alpert, M. (1990). Perceiver and poser asymmetries in processing facial emotion. *Brain and Cognition, 13,* 167-177.

Brockmeier, B., and Ulrich, G. (1993). Asymmetries of expressive facial movements during experimentally induced positive versus negative mood status: A video-analytic study. *Cognition and Emotion, 7,* 393-405.

Brodal, A. (1965). *The cranial nerves.* Oxford: Blackwell.

Brody, L.R., and Hall, J.A. (2000). Gender, emotion, and expression. In M. Lewis and J.M. Haviland (Eds.), *Handbook of emotions* (2nd ed., pp. 447-460). New York: Guilford Press.

Buck, R. (1984). *The communication of emotion.* New York: Guilford Press.

Buck, R., Baron, R., Barelette, D. (1982). The temporal organization of spontaneous non-verbal expression: A segmental analyses. *Journal of Personality and Social Psychology, 42,* 506-517.

Buck, R., Baron, R., Goodman, N., and Shapiro, N. (1980). The utilization of spontaneous nonverbal behaviour in the study of emotion communication. *Journal of Personality and Social Psychology, 39,* 522-529.

Babad, E.Y., and Wallbott, H.G. (1986). The effects of social factors on emotional reactions. In K.R. Scherer, H.G., Wallbott, and A.B. Summerfield (Eds.), *Experiencing emotion: A cross-cultural study* (pp. 154-172). New York: Cambridge University Press.

Cacioppo, J.T., and Petty, R.E. (1981). Lateral asymmetry in the expression of cognition and emotion. *Journal of Experimental Psychology: Human Perception and Performance, 7,* 333-341.

Campbell, R. (1978). Asymmetries in interpreting and expressing posed expression. *Cortex, 14,* 327-342.

——— Left handers' smiles: Asymmetries in the projection of a posed expression. *Cortex, 14,* 571-579

——— Asymmetries of facial action: Some facts and fiction of normal movement. In R. Bruyer (Ed.), *The neuropsychology of facial perception and facial expression* (pp. 247-267). Hillsdale, NJ.: Lawrence Erlbaum.

Darwin, C. (1872). *The expression of emotions in man and animals.* London: Murray.

De Jong, R.N. (1979). *The neurologic examination. New York*: Harper and Row.

Ehrlichman, H. (1987). Hemispheric asymmetry and positive-negative affect. In D. Ottoson (Ed.), *Duality and unity of the brain.* London: Macmillan.

Elfenbein, H.A., and Ambady, N. (2002). On the universality and cultural specificity of emotion recognition: A meta-analysis. *Psychological Bulletin, 128,* 203-235.

——— (2003). Cultural similarity's consequences: A distance perspective on cross-cultural differences in emotion recognition. *Journal of Cross-Cultural Psychology, 34,* 92-109.

Ekman, P. (1982). *Emotion in the human face* (2nd ed.), Cambridge: University of Cambridge Press.

——— Facial expressions of emotion: An old controversy and new findings. *Philosophical Transactions of the Royal Society of London, Series B, 335,* 63-64.

——— (1994). Strong evidence for universals in facial expressions: A reply to Russell's mistaken critique. *Psychological Bulletin, 115,* 268-287.

Ekman, P., and Friesen, W.V. (1969). The repertoire of non-verbal behaviour—categories, origins, usage and coding. *Somiotica, 1,* 49-98.

——— (1971). Constants across cultures in the face and emotion. *Journal of Personality and Social Psychology, 17,* 124-129.

——— (1975). *Unmasking the face* (pp. 135-153). Englewood Cliffs, New Jersey: Prentice Hall.

——— (1976). *Pictures of facial affect.* Palo Alto CA: Consulting Psychologists' Press.

——— (1978). *Facial action coding system: A technique for the measurement of facial movement.* Palo Alto, CA: Consulting Psychologists' Press.

Ekman, P., Friesen, W.V., O' Sullivan, M., Chan, A., Diacoyanni-Tarlatzis, I., Heider, K., *et. al.*, (1987). Universals and cultural differences in the judgments of facial expressions of emotion. *Journal of Personality and Social Psychology, 53,* 712-717.

Ekman, P., Friesen, W.V., and Tomkins, S.S. (1971). Facial Affect Scoring Technique (FAST): A first validity study. *Somiotica, 3,* 37-58.

Fisher, A.H. (1993). Sex differences in emotionality: Fact or stereotype. *Feminism and Psychology, 3,* 303-318.

Fridluand, A.J. (1991). Sociality of solitary smiling: Potentation by an implicit audience. *Journal of Personality and Social Psychology, 60,* 229-240.

——— (1994). *Human facial expression: An evolutionary view.* San Diego, CA: Academic Press.

Friesen, W.V. (1972). Cultural differences in facial expressions in a social situation: An experimental test of the concept of display rules. *Unpublished doctoral dissertation. University of California,* San Francisco.

Garner, P.W. (1996). The relations of emotional role taking, affective/ moral attributions, and emotional display rule knowledge to low income school age children's social competence. *Journal of Applied Developmental Psychology, 17,* 19-36.

Girard, E., Tassinary, L.G., Kappas, A., and Bontempo, D. (1996). A study of the ability to control precisely the contraction of muscles in different regions of the face. *Paper presented at the Thirty sixth Annual meeting of the society for Psychophysiological Research,* Vancouver, Canada.

Girard, E., Tassinary, L.G., Kappas, A., Gosselin, P., and Bontempo, D. (1997). The covert to covert threshold for facial actions: An EMG study. *Paper presented at the Thirty Seventh Annual meeting of the society for Psychophysiological Research,* Cape Cod, Massachusetts.

Graves, R., Goodglass, H. and Landis, T. (1982). Mouth asymmetry during spontaneous speech. *Neuropsychologia, 20,* 371-381.

Greenfield, P.M. (1994). Independence and interdependence as development scripts: Implications for theory, research and practice. In P.M. Greenfield and R.R. Cocking (Eds.), *Cross-cultural roots of minority child development* (pp. 1-40). Hillsdale NJ: Lawrence Erlbaum Associates Inc.

Hausmann, M., Behrendt-Koerbitz, F., Kantz, H., Lamm, C., Radelt, F., and Gûnturkun, O. (1998). Sex differences in oral asymmetries during word repetition. *Neuropsychologia, 36,* 1397-1402.

Hess, U., Banse, R., and Kappas, A. (1995). The intensity of facial expression is determined by underlying affective state and social situation. *Journal of Personality and Social Psychology, 69,* 280-288.

Hofstede, G. (1980). *Culture's Consequences.* Beverly Hills, CA: Sage.

——— (1980). Culture's Consequences. (Second Ed.), *Comparing values, behaviours, institutions, and organizations across nations.* Thousand Oaks CA: Sage.

Izard, C.E. (1971). *The face of emotion,* New York: Appleton-Century Crafts.

——— (1983). *The maximally discriminative facial movement coding system.* Instruction Resource Centre, University of Delaware, Delaware, USA.

——— (1994). Innate and universal facial expressions: Evidence from developmental and cross-cultural research: *Psychophysiological Bulletin, 115,* 228-299.

Jackobs, E., Manstead, A.S.R., and Fischer, A.H. (1999a). Social motives and emotional feelings as determinants of facial displays: The case of smiling. *Personality and Social Psychology Bulletin, 25,* 424-435.

——— (1999b). Social motives, emotional feelings and smiling. *Cognition and Emotion, 13,* 321-345.

Kagitcibasi, C. (1996). *Family and human development across cultures: A view from the other side.* Mahwah, NJ: Lawrence Earlbaum Associates, Inc.

Karch, G.R., and Grant, C.W. (1978). Asymmetries in perception of the sides of the human face. *Perceptual and Motor Skills, 47,* 727-734.

Kitayama, S., Markus, H.R., and Matsumoto, H. (1995). Culture, self, and emotion: A cultural perspective on "self-conscious" emotions. In J.P. Tangney, and K.W. Fischer (Eds.), *Self-conscious emotions: The psychology of shame, guilt, embarrassment, and pride* (pp. 439-464). New York: Guilford Press.

Knox, K. (1972). An investigation of non-verbal behaviour in relation to hemispheric dominance. *Unpublished M.A. Thesis, University of California,* San Francisco.

Kop, W.J., Merckelbach, H., and Muris, P. (1991). *Unilateral Contraction,* San Francisco.

Kowner, R. (1995). Laterality in facial expression and its effect on attributions of emotion and personality: A reconsideration. *Neuropsychologia, 33,* 539-559.

Kowner, R., and Ogawa, T. (1995). The role of rater's sex, personality, and appearance in judgements of facial beauty. *Perceptual and Motor Skills, 81,* 339-349.

Ladavas, E. (1982). The development of facedness. *Cortex, 18,* 535-545.

Lebra, T.S. (1976). *Japanese pattern of behaviour.* Honolulu: University of Hawaii Press.

Lerner, M.J. (1980). *The belief in a just world: A fundamental delusion.* New York: Plenum.

Leventhal, H.L., and Tomarken, A.J. (1986). Emotion: Today's problem. *Annual Review of Psychology, 37,* 565-610.

Levenson, R.W., Ekman, P., and Friesen, W.V. (1990). Voluntary facial action generates emotion specific autonomic nervous activity. *Psychophysics, 27,* 363-384.

Loring, D.W., Meador, K.J., Allison, J.D. and Wright, J.C. (2000). Relationship between motor and language activation using FMRI. *Neurology, 54,* 981-983.

Lynn, J.G., and Lynn, D.R. (1938). Face hand laterality in relation to personality. *Journal of Abnormal and Social Psychology, 38,* 250-276.

Madsen, M.C., and Kagan, S. (1973). Mother-directed achievement of children in two cultures. *Journal of Cross-Cultural Psychology, 4,* 221-228.

Mandal, M.K. (1987). Decoding facial emotions in terms of expressiveness by schizophrenics and depressives. *Psychiatry: Interpersonal and Biological Processes, 50*, 371-376.

Mandal, M.K., Asthana, H.S., and Biswal, R.K. (2008). Side bias in Human behaviour. In N. Srinivasan, A.K. Gupta, J. Pandey (Eds.), *Advances in Cognitive Sciences,* (pp. 135-151), New Delhi: Sage.

Mandal, M.K., and Singh, S.K. (1990). Lateral asymmetry in identification and expression of facial emotion. *Cognition and Emotion, 4,* 61-70.

Mandal, M.K., Bryden, M.P., and Bulman-Flemming, M.B. (1996). Similarities and variations in facial expression of emotion: Cross-cultural evidence. *International Journal of Psychology, 31,* 49-58.

Mandal, M.K., Harizuka, S., Bhushan, B., and Mishra, R.C. (2001). Cultural variation in hemifacial asymmetry of emotion expressions. *British Journal of Social Psychology, 40,* 385-398.

Mandal, M.K., Pandey, G., Singh, S.K., and Asthana H.S. (1992). Hand preference in India. *International Journal of Psychology, 27,* 433-442.

Markus, H.R., and Kitayama, S. (1991). Culture and the self: Implications for cognition, emotion and motivation. *Psychological Review, 98,* 224-253.

Matsumoto, D. (1989). Cultural influence on the perception of emotion. *Journal of Cross-Cultural Psychology, 20,* 92-105.

——— (1990). Cultural similarities and differences in display rules. *Motivation and Emotion, 14,* 195-214.

——— (1992). American-Japanese cultural differences in the recognition of universal facial expression. *Journal of Cross-Cultural Psychology, 23,* 72-84.

Mesquita, B. (2001). Emotions in collectivist and individualist context. *Journal of Personality and Social Psychology, 80,* 68-74.

Mesquita, B., Frijda, N.H., and Scherer, K.R. (1997). Culture and emotion. In J.W. Berry, P.R. Dasen, and T.S. Saraawathi (Eds.), *Handbook of Cross-Cultural Psychology,* (Vol. 2): *Basic processes and human development* (pp. 225-297). Boston: Allyn and Bacon.

Miehlke, A. (1973). *Surgery of the facial nerve.* Philadelphia: W.B. Saunders.

Misra, G., and Agarwal, R. (1985). The meaning of achievement: Implications for a cross-cultural theory of achievement motivation. In I. Reyes-Lagunes and Y.H. Poortinga (Eds.), *From a different perspective: Studies of behaviour across cultures* (pp. 250-266). Berwyn, IL: Swets, North America.

Murphy, G., and Murphy, L.B. (1968). *Asian Psychology.* New York: Basic Books.

Oyserman, D., Coon, H.M., and Kemmelmeier, M. (2002). Rethinking individualism and collectivism: Evaluation of theoretical assumptions and meta-analysis. *Psychological Bulletin, 128,* 3-72.

Pelto, P.J. (1968). The difference between "tight" and "loose" societies. *Transaction, 5,* 37-40.

Reissland, N. and Harris, P. (1991). Children's use of display rules in pride eliciting situations. *British Journal of Developmental Psychology, 9,* 431-435.

Rhodes, G., and Lynskey, M. (1989). Emotion in resting face: Taking sides. A reply to McGee and Skinner (1987). *British Journal of Social Psychology, 28,* 273-278.

Rinn, W.E. (1984). The neuropsychology of facial expression: A review of the neurological and psychological mechanisms for producing facial expression. *Psychological Bulletin, 95,* 52-77.

Roseman, I.J., Dhawan, N., Retteu, I.S., Naidu, R.K., and Thapa, U. (1995). Cultural differences and cross-cultural similarities in appraisals and emotional responses. *Journal of Cross-Cultural Psychology, 26,* 23-48.

Russel, J.A. (1991). Negative results on a reported facial expression of contempt. *Motivation and Emotion, 15,* 285-292.

Russel, J.A. (1994). Is there universal recognition of emotion from facial expression: A review of the cross-cultural studies. *Psychological Bulletin, 115,* 102-141.

Sackeim, H.A., Greenberg, M., Weiman, A., Gur, R.C., Hungerbuhler, J. and Geschwind, N. (1982). Functional brain asymmetry in the expression of positive and negative emotions: Lateralization of insults in cases of uncontrollable emotional outbursts. *Archives of Neurology, 19,* 210-218.

Sackeim, H.A., and Grega, D.M. (1987). Perceiver bias in the processing of deliberately asymmetric emotional expressions. *Brain and Cognition, 6,* 464-473.

Sackeim, H.A., and Gur, R.C. (1978). Lateral asymmetry in intensity of emotional expression. *Neuropsychologia, 16,* 473-481.

Sampson, E.E. (1981). Social change and the contexts of justice motivation. In M.J. Lerner and S.C. Lerner (Eds.), *The justice motive and social behaviour,* (pp. 97-124). New York: Plenum.

Schiff, B.B., and Lamon, M. (1989). Inducing emotion by unilateral contraction of facial muscles: A new look at hemispheric specialization and the experience of emotion. *Neuropsychologia, 27,* 923-935.

Schiff, B.B., and MacDonald, B. (1990). Facial asymmetries in the spontaneous response to positive and negative emotional arousal. *Neuropsychologia, 28,* 777-785.

Schuster, B., Forestellung, E., and Weiner, B. (1989). Perceiving the causes of success and failure: A cross-cultural examination of attributional concepts. *Journal of Cross-Cultural Psychology, 20,* 191-213.

Schwartz, G.F., Ahern, G.L., and Brown, S. (1979). Lateralized facial muscles response to positive and negative emotional stimuli. *Psychophysiology, 16,* 561-571.

Schwartz, G.F., Fair, P.L., Salt, P., Mandel, M.R., and Klerman, G.L. (1976). Facial muscle patterning to affective imagery in depressed and non-depressed subjects. *Science, 192,* 489-491.

Sinha, D., and Tripathi R.C. (1994). Individualism in a collective culture: A case of co-existence of opposites. In U. Kim, H. Triandis, C. Kagitcibasi, S. Choi, and G. Yoon (Eds.), *Individualism and collectivism: Query, method and application* (pp. 123-136). Thousand Oaks, CA: Sage.

Sirota, A., and Schwartz, G.E. (1982). Facial muscles patterning and lateralization during elation and depression imagery. *Journal of Abnormal Psychology, 91*, 25-34.

Skinner, M., and Mullen, B. (1991). Facial asymmetry in emotional expression: A meta-analysis of research. *British Journal of Social Psychology, 30*, 113-124.

Smith, W.H. (2000). Hemispheric and facial asymmetry: Gender differences. *Laterality, 5*, 251-258.

Smith, K.U., Smith, J.H., and Smith, W.H. (1991). Computerized research on the human face. *Electric Quarterly, 13 (1 and 2)*, 2-3, 2-4.

Snyder, M. (1974). Self-monitoring of expressive behaviour. *Journal of Personality and Social Psychology, 30*, 526-537.

Triandis, H.C. (1986). Collectivism vs. Individualism: A reconceptualization of a basic concept in cross cultural psychology. In C. Bagley and G.K. Verma (Eds.), *Personality, cognition and values: cross-cultural perspectives of childhood and adolescence* (pp. 60-95). Calgary, Canada: University of Calgary Press.

——— (1990). Theoretical concepts that are applicable to the analysis of ethnocentrism. In R.W. Brislin (Ed.) *Applied Cross-cultural Psychology* (pp. 34-55). Newbury Park, CA: Sage.

——— (1995). *Individualism and Collectivism*. Greeley, Co: Westview.

Tucker, D.M. (1981). Lateral brain function: Emotion and conceptualization. *Psychological Bulletin, 89*, 19-46.

Voyer, D. (1996). On the magnitude of laterality effects and sex differences in functional lateralities. *Laterality, 1*, 51-83.

Wallbott, H.G., and Scherer, K.R. (1988). Emotion and economic development: Data and speculations concerning the relationship between economic factors and emotional experience. *European Journal of Social Psychology, 18*, 267-273.

Wemple, C.Y., Safer, M.A., and Notarious, C.T. (1986). Display rules and facial expression: Intensity, asymmetry and type. *Paper presented at the Convention of the American Psychological Association*, Washington, D.C.

Williams, R.M. Jr. (1969). Achievement and success as value orientations. In B.C. Rosen, H.J. Crockett, and C.Z. Nunn (Eds.), *Achievement in American Society*, pp. 13-17, Cambridge, MA: Sehenkman.

Wolff, W. (1943). *The expression of personality*. New York: Harper.

Yecker, S., Borod, I.C., Brozgold, A., Martin, C., Alpert, M., and Welkowitz, I. (1999). Lateralization of facial emotional expression in Schizophrenic and depressed patients. *Journal of Neuropsychiatry and Clinical Neuroscience, 11*, 370-379.

Yamaguchi, S. (1994). Collectivism among Japanese: A perspective from the self. In U. Kim, H. Triandis, C. Kagitcibasi, S.C. Choi, and G. Yoon (Eds.), *Individualism and Collectivism: Query, method, and application*, pp. 175-188. Thousand Oaks, CA: Sage.

Zerman, J., and Garber, J. (1996). Display rules for anger, sadness, and pain: It depends on who is watching. *Child Development, 67*, 957-973.

Appendices

(1) Hand Preference Schedule

Sl. No	*Handedness*	*Right Hand*					*Left Hand*				
1.	Writing	1	2	3	4	5	1	2	3	4	5
2.	Eating	1	2	3	4	5	1	2	3	4	5
3.	Throwing a ball	1	2	3	4	5	1	2	3	4	5
4.	Lifting a bucket full of water	1	2	3	4	5	1	2	3	4	5
5.	Using a spoon to stir	1	2	3	4	5	1	2	3	4	5
6.	Keying the lock	1	2	3	4	5	1	2	3	4	5
7.	Scissors	1	2	3	4	5	1	2	3	4	5
8.	Painting	1	2	3	4	5	1	2	3	4	5
9.	Threading the needle	1	2	3	4	5	1	2	3	4	5
10.	Combing	1	2	3	4	5	1	2	3	4	5
11.	Brooming	1	2	3	4	5	1	2	3	4	5
12.	Winding a lock	1	2	3	4	5	1	2	3	4	5
13.	Screwing a nut	1	2	3	4	5	1	2	3	4	5
14.	Hammering a nail	1	2	3	4	5	1	2	3	4	5
15.	Opening the tap	1	2	3	4	5	1	2	3	4	5
16.	Switching the light	1	2	3	4	5	1	2	3	4	5
17.	Lighting a matchstick	1	2	3	4	5	1	2	3	4	5
18.	Tooth-brushing	1	2	3	4	5	1	2	3	4	5
19.	Sorting Cards	1	2	3	4	5	1	2	3	4	5
20.	Using Knife	1	2	3	4	5	1	2	3	4	5
21.	Using racket for games	1	2	3	4	5	1	2	3	4	5
22.	Unscrewing the jar	1	2	3	4	5	1	2	3	4	5

1 = NEVER 2 = RARELY

3 = OCCASIONALLY 4 = FREQUENTLY

5 = ALWAYS

(2) Personal Data

Name...

Age..Sex............. ....

Education..

Handedness..

(3) A Sample of Six Different Experimentally Manipulated Representation of Photograph Depicting Happy and Sad Emotions

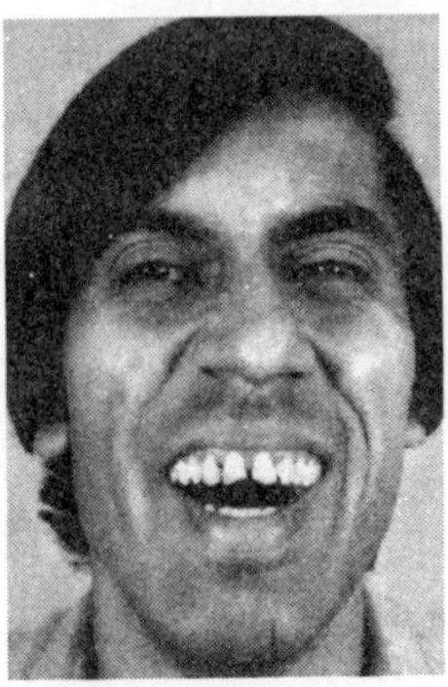

RL (HAPPY)

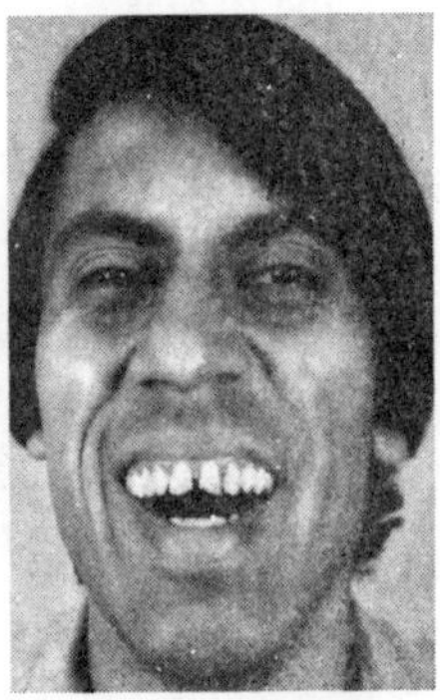

LR (HAPPY)

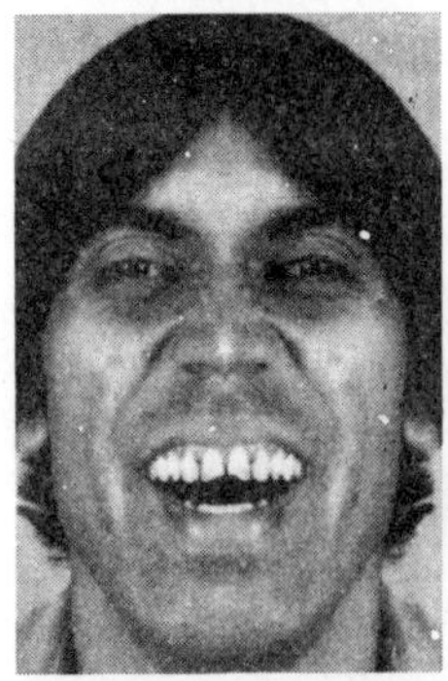

RR (HAPPY)

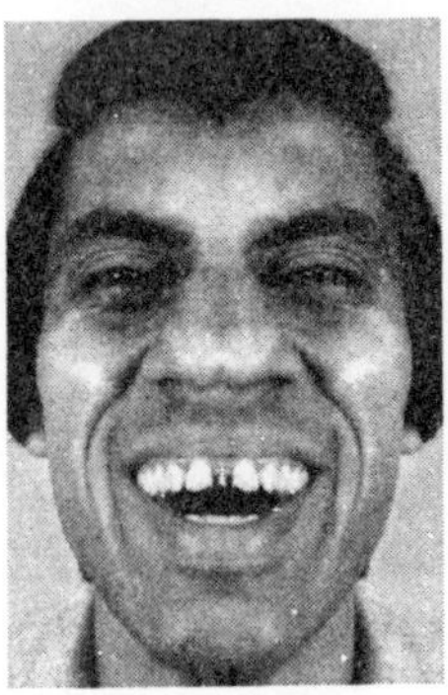

LL (HAPPY)

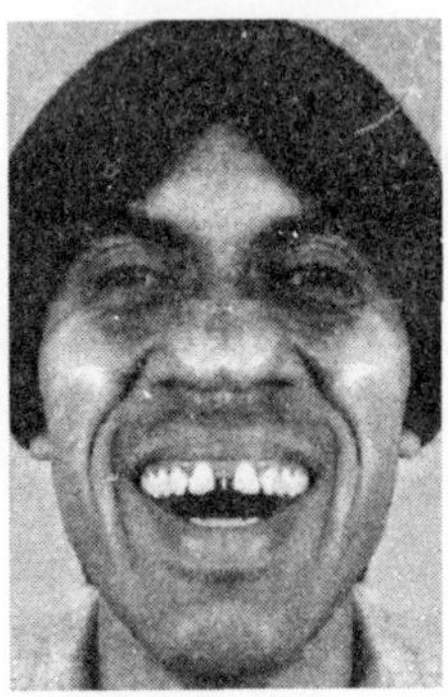

RR/LL (HAPPY)

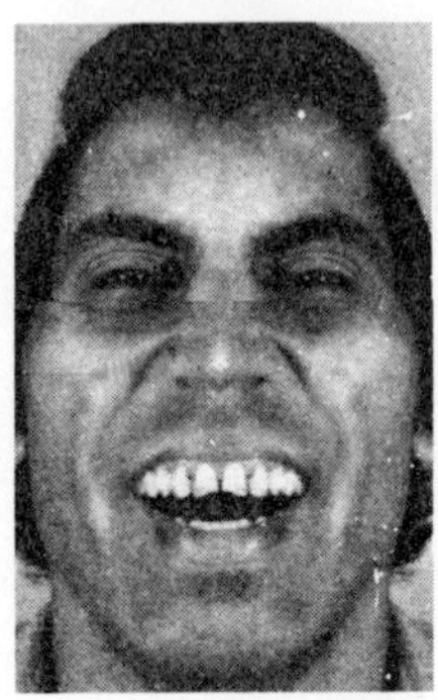

LL/RR (HAPPY)

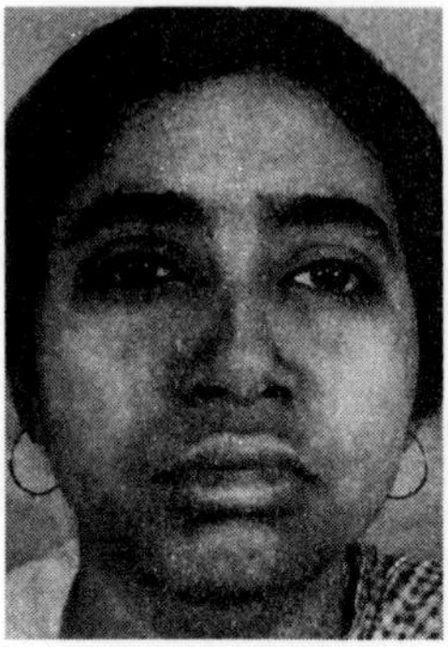

RL (SAD)

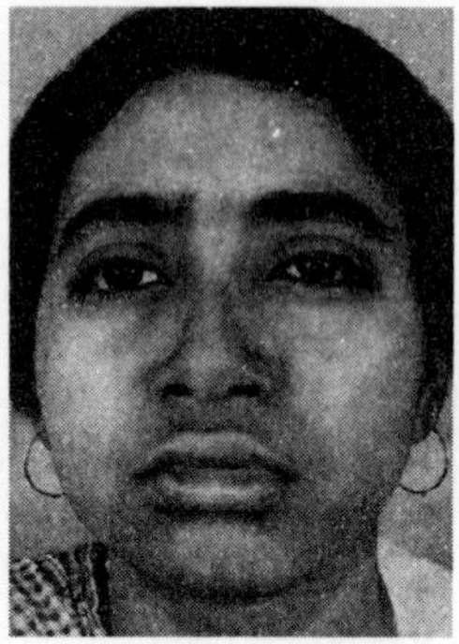

LR (SAD)

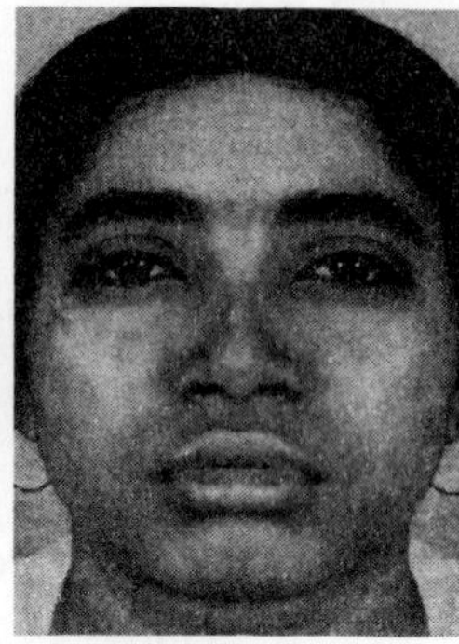

RR (SAD)

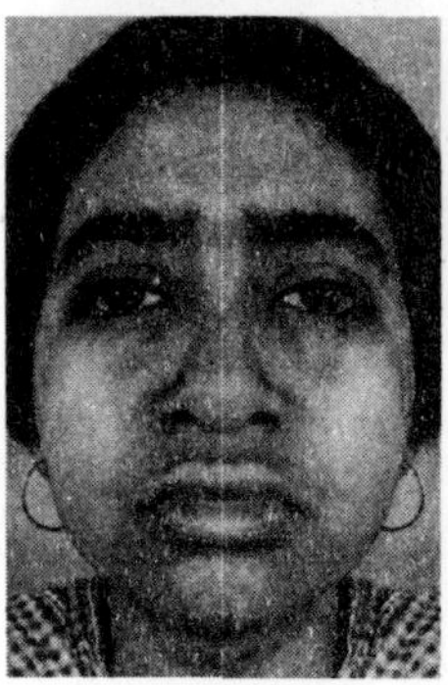

LL (SAD)

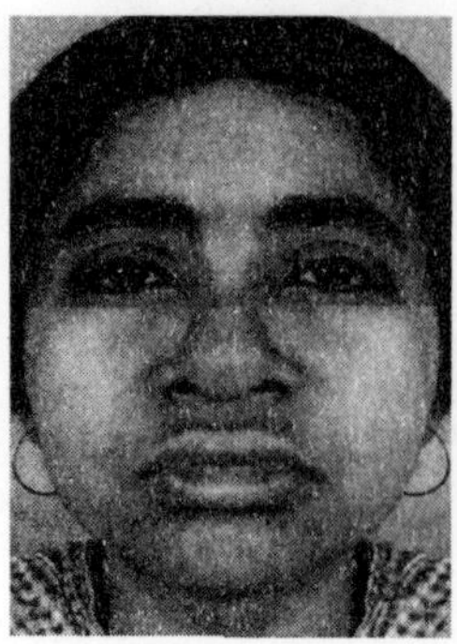

RR/LL (SAD)

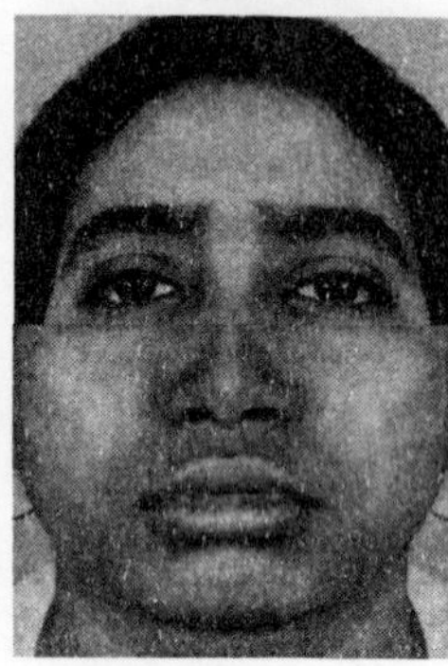

LL/RR (SAD)

Index